HAITI

POLITICS IN LATIN AMERICA
A HOOVER INSTITUTION SERIES

General Editor, **Robert Wesson**

Copublished with Hoover Institution Press,
Stanford University, Stanford, California

HAITI

Political Failures, Cultural Successes

Brian Weinstein and Aaron Segal

PRAEGER SPECIAL STUDIES • PRAEGER SCIENTIFIC

New York • Philadelphia • Eastbourne, UK
Toronto • Hong Kong • Tokyo • Sydney

Library of Congress Cataloging in Publication Data

Weinstein, Brian.
  Haiti.

  (Studies of influence in international relations)
  "Published in cooperation with the Hoover Institution,
Stanford University, Stanford, California."
  Bibliography: p.
  Includes index.
  1. Haiti. I. Segal, Aaron. II. Title. III. Series.
F1915.W45 1984   972.94   83-24501
ISBN 0-03-069869-3 (alk. paper)

568541
C

Published in 1984 by Praeger Publishers
CBS Educational and Professional Publishing,
a Division of CBS Inc.
521 Fifth Avenue, New York, NY 10175 USA

© 1984 by Praeger Publishers

456789 052 9876545321

Printed in the United States of America
on acid-free paper

In Memory of
Dr. Jean Price-Mars

A thin thread of water advanced, flowing through the plain, and the peasants went along with it shouting and singing. Antoine led them proudly beating his drum.

"Oh, Manuel! Manuel! Manuel! Why are you dead?" Délira groaned.

"No," said Annaise. She smiled through her tears. "No, he isn't dead." She took the old woman's hand and pressed it gently against her belly where the new life was stirring.

Jacques Roumain, *Masters of the Dew*
(trans. Langston Hughes, Mercer Cook)

FOREWORD

Haiti is distinctive in this hemisphere. It is the only Latin American nation of French (or French-Creole) language and culture, just as it is the only one of overwhelmingly African racial background. Haiti and Paraguay have the two remaining long-term personal dictatorships in the hemisphere, and the Haitian regime of Jean-Claude Duvalier, considerably more severe than the Paraguayan of Alfredo Stroessner, is exceptionally repressive. It amounts to "government by franchise," in the words of the authors of this monograph; this is a system of licensed exploitation, much closer kin to gangsterism than to constitutional democracy. Haiti is also exceptional in poverty; it is the poorest of Latin American countries by a wide margin. Compared to the Haitian poor, the underclasses of Colombia or even Guatemala are rather comfortably situated. Yet the Haitians are remarkably creative in their arts, music, and crafts.

In Haiti the principal problems of the less-developed world converge: shortage of arable land, overpopulation, malnutrition and chronic disease, bad government and corruption, gross inequality and separation of elite from masses, a dependent economy, lack of capital, and so forth. The recent growth of illegal migration from Haiti to the United States has brought this situation to the attention of the American public; but even if there were no black boat people, Haiti represents the kind of problem that the wealthy industrialized nations must confront for the sake of world order and the human future.

Brian Weinstein and Aaron Segal do not claim to have the answers, but they expose clearly the problems and point to some of the potentials of the future.

Robert Wesson

PREFACE

A series of books on the Caribbean and Latin America is enriched by including a volume on Haiti. Often ignored, shunned, and isolated in the course of its long history because of language, racial, or political differences with its neighbors, this black republic is one of the most complex and interesting countries in the region.

We came initially to Haiti drawn by Brian Weinstein's interest in language and Arron Segal's interest in population. These research concerns have broadened, and in the present volume we attempt to analyze the entire political system. The theme of the book is that Haiti is a political failure but a cultural success. Its political system has consistently failed to provide liberty, justice, participation, or welfare except for a privileged few. Its abandoned, exploited, and disdained peasants, whose labor permits the economy to function, have formulated and nurtured an interesting and productive culture which gave them the strength to survive while providing Haiti with a clear, well-defined national identity. Economic, ecological, and political changes threaten the system, but Haitian culture is likely to endure.

We have received much assistance in our effort to understand the failures and the successes. Albert Valdman and Charles Foster shared their extensive knowledge of Haiti and enabled us to participate in a conference, "Haiti: Present State and Future Prospects," sponsored by the Creole Institute of Indiana University and the Johnson Foundation in September 1982. Their own forthcoming book will be a valuable addition to the literature on Haiti. Many Haitians and others, who must remain anonymous, shared their knowledge and views; they are cited as "an observer."

Aaron Segal would like to thank Mats Lundahl for sharing his understanding of Haitian realities, and Thomas Mathews and Robert Anderson for first launching him into Caribbean waters.

Brian Weinstein wishes to thank Jean Dominique, agronomist and journalist, who read and commented on the manuscript, the Department of Political Science at Howard University, particularly Mildred Mason, Gwendolyn Sumlin, and Lillian Gibbs, Keith Q. Warner of the Romance Languages Department, and the Moorland Spingarn Research Center at Howard University, particularly Cornelia Stokes and J. Johnson.

Robert Wesson of the Hoover Institution and Dorothy Breitbart and Susan Goodman Alkana of Praeger Publishers shepherded this effort from manuscript to book.

Brian Weinstein
Aaron Segal

CONTENTS

HAITI

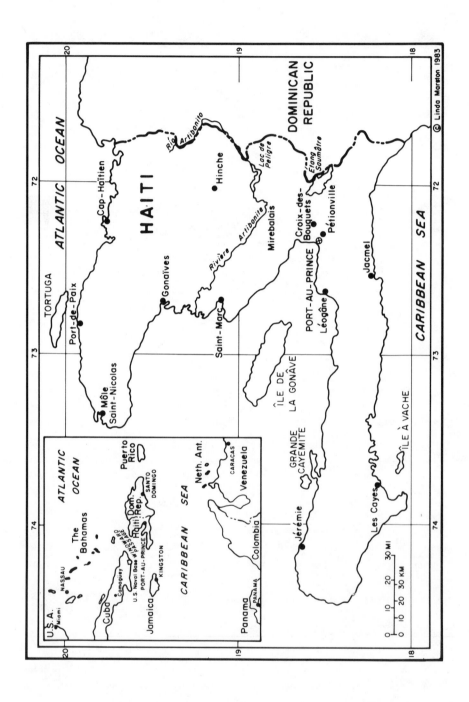

© Linda Marston 1983

1

THE TWO WORLDS OF HAITI

Haiti is two countries in one, but its long history as an independent republic and its national culture give all its people a strong, well-defined sense of identity and distinguish it from other Caribbean islands and from many other Third World countries. It is the first independent black republic in the world, and the second independent state in the Western Hemisphere. The Haitian revolution was one of the few successful slave uprisings in human history. Yet, since the time of its independence, Haiti's political history has been characterized by the division of the country into two clearly separate populations. One is the rural masses from whom has emerged an original and vibrant culture, the wellspring of Haitian identity. The other is composed of urban-based elites who have saddled the land with an immobile political order unwilling to tackle the enormous economic and social problems the country has faced from independence the morning of January 1, 1804, to the present.

Before winning its freedom Haiti was one of the richest colonies in the world; its wealth, derived from sugar, coffee, indigo, and cotton, was produced during the eighteenth century by an African slave labor force, and mostly consumed by merchants and estate owners. Now, by almost any standard of measurement, it is the poorest country in the Americas and one of the poorest on this earth.[1] Most Haitians are underfed and undernourished while the elite sector of the population eats as well as middle-class North Americans. There is little evidence that rural Haitians, still 80 percent of the population, have experienced any significant improvement in their standard of living for over one hundred years. What monetary surplus the peasants generate is siphoned off by the urban sector with its bloated military and government bureaucracy, regressive taxes and usurers, exporters, and middlemen.

The Haitian revolution freed the slaves from their shackles only to place then under the domination of a tiny national elite who maintain control over 90 percent of the people via custom, force, and marriage. This same elite, squabbling among themselves on a brown versus black basis, has since independence monopolized national political life, social status and prestige, government and military senior posts, and Haiti's slender economic surplus. It forms a world unto itself. The masses follow their own customs and culture. By trying to maintain their distance from the elites they have established a separate world which protects them against the depredations of the first world. The balance between the two Haitis is changing, however, because of elite greed, damaging agricultural practices, overpopulation, growing landlessness, and ecological changes which lower productivity and promote urbanization. Rural decline is driving the two worlds closer together and may eventually provide the impetus for a restructuring of the Haitian political system.

TWO WORLDS

The first world is French-speaking, worships in Catholic or Protestant churches, prides itself on its ties with France and European culture, does business with North Americans, and seeks to control and channel the country's contacts with the outside.[2] This first world is exploitative and paranoiac, seeing politics and economics as a zero-sum game with all the spoils to the winner and disgrace, possibly exile, or even death to the losers. This world is arbitrary, relies on patronage and coercion for control, disdains and despises democratic values, and is manipulative and hierarchical. It is male-dominated in which the senior political, military, and bureaucratic posts are held by men appointed on the basis of kinship, friendship, or proven loyalty.

While no more than 10 percent of Haitians are actors in the first world, it provides the minimal grid and infrastructure which constitutes official or legal Haiti. Here are the government ministries, the military and presidential guard, the courts, church hierarchy, the best public and religious school systems, medium and large businesses, and the extra-official secret police, thugs, and informers. This first world is dominated by the capital, sometimes called the Republic of Port-au-Prince, with a current metropolitan area swollen to about 1 million citizens, twenty times the size of any other Haitian urban area.[3] From Port-au-Prince the first world provides for military-cum-administrative control of the provinces which ensures against murmurs of dissent. This world is much better at extraction of economic surplus from the rural areas than in providing even minimal services such as roads, credit, schools, dispensaries, and running water.[4]

Most Haitians do not participate actively in this realm; they endure it fatalistically. The peasants have more than 180 years of experience in sorting out their local affairs so as to minimize government intervention. To expect nothing positive from Port-au-Prince and to take as few problems as possible to Port-au-Prince has become a deeply inured peasant strategy for survival. A variety of rural self-help measures, including the traditional shared harvesting or *coumbite* are relied on rather than the pursuit of government help. They retreat into the cultivation of subsistence crops away from cash crops too much of whose earnings go into Port-au-Prince pockets. They avoid living in concentrated settlements and choose to build their houses where they are not easily seen from the road. Peasants organize their existence to resist "the tyranny of the government and the cities."[5] Jean-Jacques Honorat, Haitian economist and agronomist, adds: "The Haitian peasant purely and simply ignores the government legislation and opposes it with an underground customary law which alone regulates intra-community relations."[6] This customary law recognizes polygamy and regulates land ownership among other important aspects of rural life.[7]

The peasants live in a second world of a deeply imbued religious faith and popular culture. It is Creole-speaking, broadly participatory, and based on rites and spectacles associated with "Voodoo."

Foreigners gave the name "Voodoo" to Haitian religion, and then they erroneously equated it with magical and exotic practices anywhere in the world, thus distorting and denigrating this rich, syncretistic religion. Alfred Métraux, noted French anthropologist, defined Voodoo simply as "An ensemble of beliefs and rituals of African origin, closely tied to Catholic practices, constituting the religion of most Haitian peasants and urban proletariat...."[8] Its origin can be traced to the eighteenth-century plantations where slaves from West and Central Africa reshaped Christianity and their own ancestral beliefs and practices to meet their new needs in Haiti. The paucity of Catholic priests and the disrepute of the few who remained after the revolution meant that during the nineteenth century Voodoo had no moral religious rival. Furthermore, baron de Vastey, writer and secretary to King Christophe, articulated the resentments of intellectuals, entrepreneurs, and others when he accused the priests of racism: "These priests would forever tell us in their sermons that whites were superior to us. . . . [9] The temples or *hounforts* dotted the countryside, not Catholic chapels. The absence of a rural administrative infrastructure throughout the nineteenth century meant that Voodoo became the primary basis of rural social organization. James Leyburn, an American sociologist, has documented its emergence as a way of life in his classic 1941 study. [10]

Today Haitians regard Catholocism and Voodoo as compatible belief systems. Officially Catholic, they practice both religions. For instance, one peasant remarked to Alfred Métraux that "one has to be Catholic to serve the loa [Voodoo spirits]." [11]

Voodoo contributes to a world seemingly the antithesis of the first. It is androgynous with male priests and female priestesses. It is open to all ages and social classes. The participants, including priests, priestesses, and their helpers, are one's neighbors and friends. The spirits are capricious but open to being propitiated. There is a wealth of ceremonies throughout the year involving music, dance, singing, crafts, food and beverage offerings, and other entertainments.

The religion's belief system evolves according to the needs of its adherents and thus offers some emotional security to Haitians constantly menaced by hunger and illness. The changing repertoire of songs, which are particular to each community or congregation, reflect fears and joys of the times and thereby provide some comfort. [12] Its social functions and cultural continuity provide Haitians with a sense of group and even national identity and well-being, as well as reinforcing family solidarity. There are also the titles, prestige, small-scale credit, folk medicine (the only medicine available to most Haitians), the chance to witness or to be possessed by a spirit, and a plausible belief system. According to Métraux, in rural areas Voodoo "gives dignity to existences that would otherwise be crushed by the hard labor of the fields and the misery." [13] In the Port-au-Prince area, as Haitian anthropologist Michel S. Laguerre has shown, acquiring expertise in Voodoo and "opening a temple are means used by urban dwellers to achieve upward mobility in their communities." [14] Protestantism, brought to the island's rural areas by North Americans, also fills these functions, but thus far Voodoo is dominant.

Out of slavery into other forms of oppression, Haitians have fashioned their own response to the cruelty of fate. It is a response that reaffirms their ties to their Haitian and African ancestors; it also gives rural society a conservative cast and has its own forms of exploitation. For this reason one should not romanticize rural life or Voodoo. Indirectly, Voodoo and rural culture support the political stagnation of the country insofar as they are a temporary refuge and they lead the peasant to believe any radical change will "dislocate his life, leaving him worse off than before."[15] The exploitation comes from the obligation each believer has toward the loa with which he identifies or from which he requests favors. Every year the believer must return to his or her home temple to make sacrifices to the spirit in the form of money and food.[16] In short, the poor are exploited. Voodoo priests and priestesses can also act to undermine efforts to change the society by using their spiritual authority to enforce political conformity. Some even work as police agents, merchants and coffee middlemen, benefiting thereby.

A material basis for the conservatism and relative stability characteristic of rural areas, at least until recently, is land ownership. Soon after independence large estates, particularly in the south, were broken up mainly for the benefit of army officers. Ordinary soldiers and former slaves settled on vacant land claiming it for themselves and their descendants. Patterns of inheritance, which, following French custom, guaranteed equal shares to all children, including those illegitimate, broke the lands up further into smaller and smaller parcels. A largely de facto land tenure system evolved which provided adult Haitians with small holdings unlike the rest of Latin America. Despite emigration toward Port-au-Prince, the Dominican Republic, and Cuba, there was little movement from department to department within Haiti. "The 1950 census revealed that no more than 2.5 percent of the population of a *département* came from outside its own borders." Ten years later the author of a study of peasant life concluded that neither methods of cultivation nor the crops chosen have changed since 1790.[17]

This stability and stagnation are one reason why there is little challenge from below to elite control. Local life has no influence on national decision making and this has been so since independence; the peasantry are politically impotent. For Mintz, "the will of the people is not heard and, given Haiti's present structure, need not be heard by those who are content to rule. This is the real problem of Haiti."[18]

There is no way most Haitians can make their needs known to the government, although apathy and distrust are forms of resistance. The adult population is 80 percent illiterate, there is a force of repression available in every district, and people are agonizingly poor. There are almost no functioning representative institutions, whether farmers' associations or peasant leagues, outside the cities. Mitigating this situation is peasant belief they own their own land, no matter how eroded or fragmented, since their ancestors are buried on or near their land. And there is a support network of beliefs, ceremonies, and friends in levels of community outside the state apparatus such as the lakou and bourg-jardin to make life bearable. It is not religion per se that is the opiate of the people in the nineteenth-century sense of Karl Marx. Haitian popular culture based on a syncretic religion, race, and a sense of identification with the land offers Haitians an alternative to pure subjugation. At the same time it is a brake on meaningful development.

Haitians have also voted with their feet against their misery. They emigrated to the Dominican Republic and Cuba for many years, but it is only since the end of World War II that emigration has rivaled refuge in the second world's culture and religion as an outlet for Haitian discontents. Counting earlier migrations to Cuba, about one million Haitians live outside the homeland compared with over five and one-half million on the island itself.[19] It is a proportion of emigrants comparable to that of most Caribbean societies during the same period but is all the more remarkable since Haiti lacks the recent colonial ties that made and make emigration easier for Jamaicans, Guadeloupans, Puerto Ricans, and others.[20]

It is hunger and malnutrition from overpopulation and declining food production, land fragmentation and erosion, and the utter indifference of the government to their plight that prompts rural Haitians to leave for the city and foreign lands. Many leave from the wind-swept villages of the northwest where periodic famines and hurricanes have caused widespread destruction. But the outpouring is generalized throughout Haiti, and the principal destinations, legal or illegal, are the Dominican Republic, the United States of America, the Bahamas, Canada, and French overseas departments in the Caribbean. Smaller numbers have arrived in France, Africa, and Latin America. The pull is the prospect of any kind of work for the unskilled and semiskilled. Loyal to friends and family as well as conscientious in repaying the loans which make the exodus possible, the Haitians abroad send proportionately huge sums of money back home. Annual estimates as high as $100 million have been made.

The loss of life and the high risks involved in leaving Haiti, especially by frail sailing vessels, have become an international scandal. No one wants the Haitian boat people. Cuba offers provisions for continuing their voyage but no sanctuary. The Bahamas government is busy trying to expel long-settled Haitians and wants no newcomers. The Dominican Republic prefers temporary workers and treats them badly. Between 1974 and 1981 about 40,000 Haitians were able to enter the United States illegally by boat, but new regulations and surveillance have since cut the numbers. American authorities granted most arrivals a "status pending" document that enable them to seek work and lodging, mostly in Miami's Little Haiti, while their requests for political asylum were being heard, but almost 2,000 were detained in camps for up to a year and a half until the force of public opinion and legal action secured their release pending hearings.

Although the plight of the refugees or migrants has raised many questions in the foreign press and in political circles about the Haitian political and economic system, there are no signs of basic change. In Haitian history those who rule do so through brute power and not by consent. Even several radical exile movements and parties tend to be elitist in thought, social composition, and action, professing to guide rather than to follow or learn from the masses.

The most important challenges to the division of Haiti into two worlds, of one exploiting the other, have come from within the country as ideas rather than political movements. An important intellectual challenge to the elites' belief in their own superiority was the work of Jean Price-Mars, the foremost Haitian thinker of this century.[21] Born in 1876 into a black, prominent northern Haitian family he was educated in France and Haiti and practiced medicine, like so many other important figures in Haitian political history. The American occupation, beginning in 1915, affronted him and forced him to reconsider the history of his country, which he had studied through the writings of historian Antenor Firmin and others.

Price-Mars articulated what many felt, namely the division of the country into two worlds. He blamed it for Haiti's weakness and political stagnation. In his lectures about elite behavior, given at St. Marc, Cap Haïtien, and Port-au-Prince in 1917, two years after the beginning of the American occupation, he analyzed the elite's indifference to Haiti, their narcissism and selfishness. But, his general message is that the posturing and destructive behavior could be changed through self-awareness and will.[22]

Partly in order to draw these two worlds together he initiated a series of ethnographic studies in the 1920s through which he encouraged urban elites to examine the ways of their rural and poor countrymen and women. In his publications, public speeches, and training of enthusiastic followers of all colors, Price-Mars affirmed proudly Haiti's African roots. His version of Negritude, a doctrine of the cultural unity, originality, and pride of African peoples wherever their place of residence, was put forth in his book, *Ainsi parla l'oncle*. Published in 1928, it had enormous intellectual appeal in francophone Africa, Haiti, France, and the French-speaking Antilles.

By means of this volume Price-Mars intellectually legitimized the second world by asking and answering the following question:

> Does Haitian society have a background of oral traditions, legends, tales, songs, riddles, customs, observances, ceremonies and beliefs which are characteristic of it or that it has assimilated so as to give them its personal imprint? And if this folklore exists, what is its value from the literary and scientific point of view?[23]

The black intellectual and his black and brown protégés answered the first question in the affirmative and then explained the value of Haitian culture through their novels and ethnographic writings down to the present. They were able to help elite Haitians discover their own national culture and to take justifiable pride in it, thus creating the indigenist cultural movement. In his preface to *La montagne ensorcelée (Bewitched Mountain)* published in 1931 by a talented young friend Jacques Roumain, Price-Mars articulated the connection between Haitian intellectuals and peasants. He explained that the Haitian peasants had created a new religion out of Christianity and African religions and that the writer could put into words the effect of that syncretism on Haiti. The intellectual would articulate the folk spirit into a "Haitian esthetic."[24] In his great novel, *Masters of the Dew (Gouverneurs de la rosée)* Roumain tried to do just that. He drew upon peasant language and Voodoo as he dissected his society showing the petty and mean conflicts among peasants, the indifference of government and then the triumph of love and unity in building a better life. One Trinidadian critic summarized this work well: "Roumain's work easily transcends the vision of despair so frequently found in the Caribbean novel of protest and is perhaps the first to present the Haitian and, by analogy, Caribbean landscape with this sense of elation and poetic wonder."[25] A radical exile poet, René Depestre, wrote as recently as 1980 that Price-Mars's work—directly or indirectly through Roumain and others—made peasant throught and art "a conscious part of Haitian realities."[26]

Price-Mars's lifelong effort to bridge the two worlds intellectually was racially and politically distorted and manipulated by others, including a future president, Dr. François Duvalier. Political leaders took some of these ideas for their own in the 1940s and 1950s; a few twisted them into a nationalist-racialist apology for favoring black over brown-skinned elites, without regard for the masses.[27] Obsessions with racial identity and the revolution against France obscured the real social problems based on class behavior and on Haiti's present place in the world. Indifference to peasant problems, especially erosion, deforestation, and Creole culture started an ecological and human disaster threatening both worlds.

Haiti: The Land

Geographically, Haiti occupies the western and most ruggedly mountainous one-third of the island of Hispaniola. As a result of a series of nineteenth-century wars, including a 20 year Haitian invasion and occupation of the Dominican Republic, a Dominican counterattack, and later negotiations, the 180 mile (300 km) north-south boundary between the two states is fixed and not contested today.[28] The Dominican Republic, with a population over 5 million, has two-thirds of the island and an even greater share of its arable land and mineral and other natural resources.

Politics and historical experience, rather than geography, have served to divide these two republics. Although the border area itself is semiarid, sparsely populated, and partly desolate, it is easily traversed on foot. There are a few roads, but numerous roadblocks and frequent police and military patrols on both sides can discourage legitimate traffic and trade, except for Haitian contract labor for Dominican sugar estates from which both governments profit. Conflict, conquest, and war have fueled nationalist sentiments in each country, as has frequent past harboring of political exiles. The cultural, color, and language differences have become significant and are reinforced by political intrigue, distrust, and jealousy.

Haiti itself including its small offshore islands of La Tortue, la Gonâve, Ile de la Vache, Les Cayemites, and La Navase is about the size of Maryland or 10,714 square miles. Topographically, people say it resembles a crumpled piece of paper divided into three mountain ranges crossed by north-south river valleys. The highest point is La Selle Peak over 8,000 feet high; one-third of the country lies between the tropical lowlands and the mountains. There are few beaches or deep-water ports, and the major tropical forest had been cut down by the end of the nineteenth century.[29]

There are three basic geographical divisions: northern Haiti with its port at Cap Haïtien, fierce tradition of independence going back to the Kingdom of Henri Christophe (1806–1820) and its coffee and sisal; central Haiti with the plains of the Artibonite River and the commercial and government capital of Port-au-Prince; and the south with its ports and markets at Jacmel and Les Cayes and its memories of being an independent republic under President Alexandre Pétion (1806–1821).

Internationally, Haiti sits roughly midway in the 2,000 mile archipelago of islands stretching across the Caribbean Sea from the Bahamas in the north to Trinidad and Tobago in the south. Haiti's island neighbors to the west are Cuba, and the Turks and Caicos chain to the north. Haiti is 50 miles from the coast of Cuba at the nearest point, 130 miles from Jamaica, 600 from Florida, and 900 from Trinidad.

Haitian cultural geography is characterized by a skillful blending of African, Native American, and European elements. Mintz writes: "The crops Haitian peasants cultivate include the maize, sweet potato, and manioc of the indigenous Native American (Taino) people, and other cultigens which had been domesticated in aboriginal America such as papaya and the avocado; items from Oceania such as taro and mangoes; sesame and sugar cane, which originated in the Middle East and India; and vegetables from Europe. Their domestic animals, including cattle, swine, and fowls, are nearly all from the Old World. The chief agricultural tools— hoe, billhook and dibble, which are well adapted to Haiti's shallow topsoil and hilly terrain—may be European or African in origin. . . ."[30]

Climate has made the peasants' island life even more difficult. The location of the country between 69⁰ and 74⁰ longitude west makes it a clear target during the annual September to December Caribbean hurricane season. During recent years it has been severely hit. Southern Haiti is particularly vulnerable and has been frequently battered. Northwest Haiti is particularly susceptible to periodic droughts.

Adequate rainfall is a constant problem. When it rains the torrential downpours worsen the problem of soil erosion. Summers can be hot and humid with fierce tropical rains. Winters can be dry, parched, and menaced by hurricanes. The crop cycle, agriculture labor, and many other activities center around the wet and dry seasons, normally April to October, and November to March. However, due to the mountains, the prevailing winds, and other factors, the amount of annual rainfall can vary considerably within Haiti as the Central Plateau and other windward regions receive 56 inches (1400 mm) a year or more while the drought-stricken northwest peninsula receives 40 inches (1000 mm) or less.[31]

If too much or not enough rain is a problem, the soil is a nightmare for much of Haiti is hilly and rocky. Less than 30 percent of the total area of the country consists of land with a slope of less than 10 percent. Firewood is the only available combustible to most Haitians in a country which has no known commercial deposits of any fuel. Deforestation combined with runoffs, steep and increasingly cultivated hillsides, and some of the highest rural population densities in the world (almost "700 people per every square kilometer of arable land")³² has brought about devastating erosion.

In the absence of government measures to reverse the disaster, soil erosion is threatening to destroy the bases of the second world. Every year there are more Haitians and less arable land as centuries of accreted topsoil are washed away. With it are disappearing the bases of traditional culture, rural conservatism, and stability.

The Past

Energy crisis, ecological disaster, population pressure, soil erosion, oppressive governments, and a vibrant traditional culture of music, plastic arts, religion, and oral literature are the principal features of Haiti in the late twentieth century. What are the historical forces that have produced this exceptional land and society? History is more of a living presence in Haiti than in any other island of the Caribbean.

Proto-history or archaeology is still in its infancy on the island of Hispaniola but the few sites excavated have yielded striking results. There is evidence of continuous habitation as far back as 3000 B.C.³³ Present theories suggest that successive waves of Amerindian groups from the areas of what is now Guyana on the northern mainland of South America paddled their way up the Caribbean archipelago. These were primarily fisher and hunter groups who also gathered edible plants. They possibly spoke related languages and sought in the islands more abundant food supplies than were available on the mainland.

The Taino Indians who inhabited Hispaniola at the time of Columbus's first voyage in 1492 were already partly settled. They had begun to domesticate and cultivate foods such as manioc; they lived in established villages, produced pottery, wove cloth from cotton, used hammocks for sleeping, and may have numbered as many as 600,000 or as few as 60,000 when Columbus touched the shore.³⁴ Fifty years later they were extinct, killed off by forced labor, European diseases, loss of their homeland and way of life. Their heritage continues in the form of words such as "Haiti" itself which means mountainous, in their agricultural and fishing practices, and possibly in a few of their deities absorbed by Vodoo.

Columbus's claim permitted Spain to rule the whole island from 1492 to 1697. Santo Domingo became the capital city and for 50 years or more

dominated the Caribbean as its principal port. The colony attracted settlers, but its economic rationale swiftly altered. The pursuit of gold and
other precious metals brought meager results on Hispaniola itself although
it contributed to the extermination from forced labor of the Indians. Cattle ranching on open ranges for hides and beef took advantage of empty
grasslands but did not bring the sudden wealth sought by the Conquista-
dores. Instead, Santo Domingo became a staging base and garrison, first
for Spanish expeditions and eventual settlement of Cuba and Puerto Rico,
and by 1519 for the epic expedition of Cortes to Mexico.

The opening up of Mexico transformed Santo Domingo but not Hispaniola. As a port of transhipment Santo Domingo prospered from the
Mexico to Spain trade. The need to protect the heavy and slow Spanish
galleons from Caribbean piracy increased the importance of Santo Domingo as a source of provisions and a naval and military garrison. What
forced labor in Hispaniola had not completed was finished off by the export of the remaining Taino Indians to work and die in the Mexican mines.

Yet these momentous events had little effect on most of the island. The
rapid extinction of most of the Indians prompted the first official import
of African slaves in 1510. Brought primarily from West and Central Africa
(especially what is today Benin, formerly Dahomey), the Africans were
initially used in the quickly played-out gold mines and then on the first
sugar cane estates. The cultivation of sugar cane arrived in Hispaniola via
the Dutch and Jews in northeast Brazil and on the island of Curaçao.
Sixteenth-century Spain lacked the interest, capital, technology, and
markets to produce sugar effectively; the mineral wealth of Mexico and
Peru could be more easily scooped from the ground.

Thus, slavery and sugar slowly grew but did not mature under Spanish
rule. Much of Hispaniola was unoccupied; especially the mountainous
west. Just as Sir Francis Drake and his English freebooters sacked Santo
Domingo in 1588, so did French pirate bands begin in the 1620s to use
the convenient island of Tortue as a base. The buccaneers, as they came
to be known, raided the Spaniards and feuded among themselves until
1697.

That year, when France took possession of its part of the island under
the provisions of the Treaty of Ryswick, the boundary was drawn considerably to the west of its present lines. The French were quick to establish
a mainland administration in what they called Saint Domingue to lure settlers of all kinds with generous land grants and to institutionalize African
slavery. According to the calculations of historian Philip Curtin, in the century of French control 789,700 slaves were brought into the colony making

it the most important slave-importing island in the whole Caribbean, leading its nearest rival, Jamaica, by 125,000 persons.[35] Thus the colony prospered above all others.

The practice of mercantilism which assured a monoply of trade for French-owned vessels, low taxes, sure French consumers, and the protection of the French navy guaranteed a market for Saint Domingue's sugar. First a luxury for European palates, the French developed it into an opiate of the poorly nourished and rapidly growing urban dwellers of Paris and Marseilles. Slavery was rationalized theologically here as elsewhere by the clergy and economically by the planters who had found that white-indentured and forced labor could not compete with African stoop labor in a tropical climate on subsistence rations.

Colonial prosperity was achieved at a high price. So harsh was the system that slave fertility was well below replacement, calling constantly for new imports. There were periodic slave uprisings and escapes. Runaway slaves known as *marrons* fled to the mountains and established village societies. François Macandal, a one-armed slave, fled and with his companions held off the French from 1751 to 1758. Others won and kept their freedom even longer.

Another threat to white rule came from the offspring of French fathers and black mothers, many of whom were freed and educated. These mulatto men and women, called "affranchis" and "hommes de couleur" regarded themselves as Frenchmen and Frenchwomen of color; some of them, too, owned slaves and estates and chafed at the legal and informal restraints imposed by the whites. Some black slaves were also free because they had bought or had won their freedom. On the eve of the French Revolution in 1789 it has been estimated there were nearly 30,000 free mulattoes and blacks, about 40,000 whites, and around half a million slaves.[36] The poor whites in particular sought to retain discrimination based on color.

The storming of the Bastille in Paris unleashed desires and fears of change in the colonies. Freedmen and women desired equality with the whites, slave leaders wished for a stricter slave structure, while some whites supported the monarchy but others supported change. The clash of interests due to events in France, the declaration of freedom for all slaves in Haiti in 1793, and attacks by the British and Spanish contributed to the confusion and growing conflict in Saint Domingue, culminating in a revolution which devastated the countryside and destroyed slavery and the plantation system.

Revolution began in 1791 with a spontaneous slave insurrection in the north organized by Boukman, a slave and Voodoo priest. He and his followers were killed and captured but not until they had killed many slave owners.[37] At the same time the affranchis had begun their agitation for full rights in a more peaceful way by letters and petitions, but their leaders, Vincent Ogé and J.B. Chavannes, were tortured and killed by the whites.

Out of the chaos a heroic figure emerged and took charge. Toussaint Louverture was born a slave in 1743. Although he did not support the initial uprising in 1791, he joined a group of former slaves led by Jean-François Biassou and quickly took the lead. Believing that an alliance with Spain would ensure freedom for the slaves he called for support on August 29, 1793:

> Brothers and friends. I am Toussaint L'Ouverture, my name is perhaps known to you. I have undertaken vengeance. I want Liberty and Equality to reign in San Domingo. I work to bring them into existence. Unite yourselves to us, brothers, and fight with us for the same cause. . . .[38]

In 1794 he shifted his allegiance to the new French republic fighting against the Spanish and the British. Long campaigns marked by innovative military tactics allowed him to consolidate his forces and to rout the opposition. He took the Spanish city of Santo Domingo in 1801, becoming the undisputed leader of the whole island, but he made no declaration of independence.

Toussaint organized a military administrative system for the island and called for a constituent assembly in 1801 which prepared a constitution. The document named him governor general for life. Faced with economic collapse he arranged for the state to take plantations abandoned by their white and mulatto owners and to lease them to senior army officers and government officials. Guaranteed modest wages, quarters, and medical care, the former slaves were to be refixed as tenants on the land, no longer free to move about at will. In short, he was the first Haitian leader to institute forced labor.

The rise of a black leader acting on his own initiative was unacceptable to Napoleon who was preparing to re-establish slavery. Profiting from a momentary peace in Europe, the French emperor launched a massive naval invasion in 1802 to reassert absolute French control over Saint Domingue. At first the superior French forces rolled back the blacks, and through a ruse they captured and exiled Toussaint in 1802. Toussaint's lieutenant, Jean-Jacques Dessalines, took up the leadership and at the battle of La Crête-à-Pierrot broke the French stranglehold. The war continued without mercy for black, brown, and white. Yellow fever aided Dessalines and his second in command, mulatto Alexandre Pétion, by killing his French adversary, Admiral Leclerc. The atrocities committed by French troops under Leclerc's successor, General Donatien Rochambeau, and the dread of re-enslavement brought unity to the blacks and browns. With the disappearance of the metropolitan settlers who died or fled, and the death of 55,000 French soldiers and sailors from the revolutionaries' weapons and disease, Napoleon's image of a New World Empire was forever shattered. What had begun as a slave uprising ended on January 1, 1804, with the declaration of independence of "Haiti," the Indian name chosen by Dessalines who also created the nation's new flag by ripping the white from the French tricolor.

Independence and After

The blue and red flag flew over a land whose prospects were grim. Economic destruction, a hostile slaveholding world, the absence of political experience, uneasy relations between mulattoes, most of whom had been born free, and blacks, most of whom has been born slaves, along with threats from an important French military presence in the east, gave the country a poor start. Anthropologist Sidney Mintz has correctly written: "Surely the wonder. . . is not that it has fared badly, but that it has fared at all."[39]

The first threat to the new state's stability was the fear of foreign intervention. Napoleon had already sent his troops once. And when Dessalines ordered in January 1804 that whites be killed, many feared the European powers would react. The second and greater threat came in 1806 with the assassination of Dessalines, who had proclaimed himself Emperor Jacques I, and the subsequent division of the country into two separate states, north and south. Henri Christophe, a black exslave military leader born in the English colony of St. Kitts, ruled the north as king. A master builder and administrator, he had constructed Sans Souci palace and the magnificent La Ferrière fortress inland from Cap Haïtien where he feared a French invasion. The king organized a national gendarmerie, recruiting 4,000 Dahomeyans, and he used coercion and forced labor to return some of the estates and plantations to productivity. He organized an educational system designed to form skilled workers and sought technical assistance from England. For foreigners his notoriety was based on his delusions of grandeur for he created an elaborate court complete with nobility. At his, death in 1820 his kingdom and his methods of rule disappeared because the people despised them.

General Alexandre Pétion, president of the republic in the southern part of the country, was the able second lieutenant of Dessalines. Fair in color, born a free man, well-educated, and a former resident of France, he distributed land to the military rather than attempt to reconstitute the more efficient large estates. A parliament catered only to the new elites, and the shareout of land produced a small-holders' republic less prosperous than the northern kingdom. The conflicts between Christophe and Pétion institutionalized the competition between brown and black elites, but they agreed that Haiti must be free. To that end they both lent support to the Spanish, who succeeded in retaking Saint Domingo from the French.

At the death of Pétion in 1818 the head of the presidential guard, Jean-Pierre Boyer was elected president in Port-au-Prince, and two years later with the death of King Christophe he united north and south. Boyer's twenty-five years in power are the longest of any single head of state in Haiti's history. He also invaded Santo Domingo and the entire island was united under his rule from 1822 to 1843, the last time "Quisqueya," the Indian name for the whole island, was politically one. Despite his quarter-century rule, Boyer is not considered a beneficent leader by historians. Brown elites ruled at the expense of others, especially the peasants. Education was a prize guarded for a privileged few in the cities. A Rural Code was issued in 1826 strengthening government authority and used to further elite claims. He won recognition of Haitian independence by France but at the price of a crippling financial indemnity.

A combination of regional and restive elite forces deposed Boyer in 1843. In 1844 the Dominicans ousted their Haitian rulers, and after four years of what historian Dorsainvil calls "ephemeral governments," another strong figure emerged. Faustin Soulouque, the black commander of the presidential guard was elected president of Haiti in 1847. In 1849 a new constitution transformed the republic into an empire, and Soulouque took the title of Emperor Faustin I. Under the new emperor the government had the monoply of cotton and coffee exports giving it an important source of revenue, but waste and corruption emptied the treasury. Faustin favored black advancement, at least in urban areas, and supported Voodoo priests. His invasion of the eastern part of the island to reunite the two countries failed miserably, and, blaming his subordinates, the emperor had many of them killed. One of his generals, Nicolas Geffrard, fearing for his own life, led a revolt, and became president in 1859, when Soulouque sailed into exile.

Geffrard was the first president born after the revolutionary wars. He ruled from 1859 to 1867 and is praised by historians for his accomplishments. In 1860 he signed a concordat with the Vatican making Roman Catholicism the state religion and, more important, bringing Catholic educational institutions and teachers to the island. The United States government recognized his government. He created lycees, gave scholarships to study in Europe, and set up a shortlived technical school. He encouraged local agriculture and coastal shipping, but corruption and the indiscriminate printing of money seriously weakened the economy. A revolt in the north, which led Geffrard to unsuccessfully seek the help of the British, weakened him and not even the elite military unit he had created could save him.

The president sailed into exile as his predecessor had done. A bloody civil war ensued for three years pitting region against region and marked the appearance of peasant mercenary bands, the *Cacos,* who generally served the interests of northern claimants to power. (They were to play a more important role in Haitian history than the "piquets" or peasant groups in the south who opposed governments as well.) The period 1871 through 1881 was another decade of confusion, what one may call "de-institutionalization" because central institutions deteriorated as political factions, given the name of "parties", ruled the streets with gun and machete. Black versus brown racial conflicts surfaced and often coincided with regional differences, the south having a primarily brown leadership.

This was also a period of incipient major power interest in Haiti. German trading houses opened Port-au-Prince branches, and the German navy cruised Haitian waters. France remained the principal creditor and source of elite culture and language. The United States Senate, by a vote of 28 to 28, blocked the attempt by President Grant in 1870 to annex Santo Domingo, but U.S. interests in the Caribbean continued to grow.

In 1879 another strong personality took power, Lysius Salomon, a black man who had been Emperor Faustin's Minister of Financial Affairs. Dynamic and well-informed, Salomon sought to play off France, Britain, and the United States. His domestic programs included expanded public education, improved financial administration, public works, and other measures. His desire to extend his term of office beyond the prescribed date of 1886 led to insurrection and exile in 1888. Despite his failures, Salomon is regarded as one of the formidable leaders of independent Haiti.

The period from 1888 to 1915 was one of chaos and tragedy for Haiti, the prelude to another period of authoritarian rule under an American occupation force. These 27 years were filled with constant plots and revolts, foreign investments, mounting foreign financial pressures, and indifference to the rural areas. German warships humiliated the Haitian government over the treatment of a German citizen, and the American navy put pressures on the government to cede the Môle St. Nicolas, a natural deep water port on the northwest coast. France played the role of major creditor, but the National City Bank of New York pushed its way into a partnership in the new Haitian National Bank. What little economic progress that took place was confined to Port-au-Prince and the elites.

The first century of independence left Haiti with a legacy of economic stagnation, social conservatism, a corrupt and disorganized army, but a basis for unity as well: a land tenure system based on individual small holdings, Creole as a national but unofficial language, and a Voodoo religion shared by most.

By 1915 patterns in Haitian politics had also emerged clearly. In the 111 years between independence and occupation the first world ruled the second the way pirates control a captured ship. In this system of pirate politics the black and brown families at the top of the political and economic systems extracted as much as they could from their victims, the peasants of the second world; their greed was unrestrained, partly because they felt no sense of shared identity with the masses, and partly because they felt that they must maximize their profits while holding power. Meanwhile, the peasants, who realized they could expect no benefits from their rulers, sought ways to limit the depredations and protect themselves from the worst. Poor systems of communication permitted isolation and limited central government control while favoring regional leaders who, supported by friends and neighbors, threatened revolt. Although Haiti's original revolutionaries battled in the name of universalist principles of freedom, equality, and justice, the military men who sought and won power during the first century were moved more by the attractions of personal gain and did little to hide that fact. Thus, the political system located mainly in Port-au-Prince produced president after president overthrown regularly from within narrow elite ranks. This instability, increasing foreign interests, and events elsewhere in the Caribbean opened the door to U.S. intervention.

NOTES

1. Mats Lundahl, *Peasants and Poverty* (New York: St. Martin's Press, 1979).

The World Bank classifies Haiti among the 20 poorest nations in the world, and the poorest in the Western Hemisphere.

2. James G. Leyburn, *The Haitian People* (New Haven: Yale University Press, 1966), new Introduction by Sidney Mintz. Leyburn's book published in 1941 was the first systematic effort to document elite-peasant relations.

3. The first results of the 1982 Haitian census are expected to be released late in 1983. They are expected to confirm the rapid growth of Port-au-Prince and the stability of the other departments. Personal Correspondence, Patricia S. Gibson, Population and Health Officer, U.S. Embassy, Port-au-Prince, December 15, 1982.

4. US/AID/Haiti, "Country Development Strategy FY 1983-1987," mimeographed (Port-au-Prince, Jan. 1981).

5. Paul Moral, *Le paysan haïtien* (Paris: G. Maisonneuve, 1961), p. 235.

6. Jean-Jacques Honorat, *Enquête sur le développement* (Port-au-Prince: Imprimerie Centrale, 1974), p. 219.

7. Ibid, p. 220.

8. Alfred Métraux, *Le vaudou haïtien* (Paris: Gallimard, 1968), p. 117. Authors' translation.

9. Cited by J. Michael Dash, *Literature and Ideology in Haiti 1915-1961* (Totowa, New Jersey: Barnes and Noble, 1981), p. 4.

10. Leyburn, *The Haitian People,* pp. 131-65.

11. Métraux, *Le vaudou haïtien,* p. 287. Authors' translation.

12. Ibid, p. 322.

13. Ibid.

14. Michel S. Laguerre, *Voodoo Heritage* (Beverly Hills: Sage, 1980), p. 143.

15. Leyburn, *The Haitian People,* p. 9.

16. Interview, Jean Dominique, 31 May 1983.

17. Mats Lundahl, "Peasant Strategies for Dealing with Population Pressure: The Case of Haiti," in *Ibero Americana: Nordic Journal of Latin American Studies* 10 (1981): 24. And, citing a study by John M. Street and Mats Lundahl, "The State of Spatial Economic Research on Haiti: A Selective Survey," in *Anthropologica* 22 (1980): 142.

18. Sidney W. Mintz, *Caribbean Transformations* (Chicago: Aldine, 1974), p. 301.

19. James Allman, John May, "Fertility, Mortality, Migration and Family Planning in Haiti," *Population Studies* 33 (1982): 505-721.

20. See *Caribbean Review* 11 (Winter 1982). This is a special issue on the Caribbean exodus; it includes articles on Haitian emigration by Alex Stepick and Thomas D. Boswell.

21. Jacques C. Antoine, *Jean Price-Mars and Haiti* (Washington, D.C.: Three Continents Press, 1981).

22. Jean Price-Mars, *La vocation de l'élite* (Port-au-Prince: Imprimerie Edmond Chenet, 1919), pp. 87-90.

23. Antoine, *Price-Mars and Haiti,* p. 136.

24. Jean Price-Mars, "Preface," in *La montagne ensorcelée,* Jacques Roumain (1931, reprinted., Port-au-Prince: Ateliers Fardin, n.d.), pp. 9-13.

25. Dash, *Lit. Ideology in Haiti* p. 152

26. René Depestre, *Bonjour et adieu à la négritude* (Paris: Robert Lafont, 1980), p. 46.

27. David Nicholls, *From Dessalines to Duvalier: Race, Colour and National Independence in Haiti* (Cambridge: Cambridge University Press, 1979), pp. 170–71, 232–47.

28. For a general history of relations between the two see Rayford W. Logan, *Haiti and the Dominican Republic* (New York: Oxford, 1968).

29. Georges Anglade, *L'espace haïtien* (Montreal: Editions des Alizes, 1981), pp. 2–12.

30. Mintz, *Caribbean Transformations,* pp. 268–69.

31. Anglade, *L'espace haïtien,* pp. 12–19.

32. USAID/Haiti, *Country Program Overview* (Port-au-Prince and Washington: USAID, October 1982), p. 4.

33. The Museum of Man in Santo Domingo has pioneered archaeological research in Hispaniola, including sites near the Haitian border. Its publications in Spanish include its *Boletin* and various books and monographs. Carolos Esteban Deive, *El Indio, el Negro, y la Vida Tradicional Dominicana* (Santo Domingo: Museo del Hombre, 1978).

34. For the 600,000 estimate see Maurice de Young, "Profile of the North West," report prepared for USAID, Haiti, September-November 1981, p. 17. For smaller estimates see Deive, *El Indio,* and Julia Tavares, *Guide to Caribbean Pre-history* (Santo Domingo: Museo del Hombre, 1978).

35. Philip Curtin, *The Atlantic Slave Trade: A Census* (Madison: University of Wisconsin Press, 1969), p. 216.

36. "Haiti," in *Population Policies in the Caribbean* ed. Aaron Lee Segal, (Lexington, Mass: D.C. Heath, 1975). And Ivan Beghin, W. Fougère, K. King, *L'alimentation et la nutrition en Haïti* (Paris: Presses Universitaires de France, 1971), p. 29.

37. J.C. Dorsainvil, *Manuel d'historie d'Haïti* (Port-au-Prince: Frères de l'Instruction Chrétienne, 1934), pp. 68–139 for a more detailed account of events from 1791 to 1804. See also Robert Debs Heinl, Jr., and Nancy Gordon Heinl, *Written in Blood: The Story of the Haitian People, 1492–1971,* (Boston: Houghton Mifflin, 1978).

38. C.L.R. James, *The Black Jacobins: Toussaint L'Ouverture and the San Domingo Revolution,* 2nd ed. (New York: Ramdom House-Vintage, 1963), p. 125.

39. Mintz, *Caribbean Transformations,* p. 263.

2

FROM U.S. OCCUPATION TO
DUVALIER FAMILY RULE

Occupation by the United States of America from 1915 to 1934 rep-
resented a truncated, incomplete, and unsuccessful second chapter of colonial rule for Haiti, contrasting with the more productive British and
French imperial effort during the same period in the Caribbean and Africa.
Unlike the French and British, who planned to remain indefinitely in their
possessions, the Americans agreed from the start to leave by 1936.
Although occupation authorities rewrote the Haitian constitution to favor
United States commercial and business interests, and encouraged corporations to invest in order to strengthen the American presence, private sector response was timid. Washington was also reluctant to spend U.S. tax
money in Haiti.

Nonetheless, the American political presence, like the British and
French presence elsewhere, had an influence on the expansion of foreign
economic interests as well as on the local political, social, and military situation. New patterns of elite formation and a sharpened black consciousness emerged in direct or indirect reaction to white domination. And, most
important, the Americans successfully completed what other imperial
powers called the "pacification" of the colony. In Haiti that process meant
suppression of the Caco movements and the unification of the country
under one government in Port-au-Prince thereby helping to prepare the way

for the type of centralized state which later emerged. Despite vicissitudes in the relationships between the United States and Haiti since the withdrawal of the marines in 1934, U.S. governmental and nongovernmental interests have been and remain the most important foreign influences on Haiti.

OCCUPATION

At the beginning of the twentieth century fear of European influence in the Caribbean grew among U.S. policy makers and military strategists. A future canal in Central America providing a shortened sea link between the eastern and western United States would need protection as would increasing U.S. investments. Corrupt, unstable, and heavily indebted governments in the Caribbean area were an invitation to foreign intervention, particularly by the Germans. In Cuba, where U.S. investments had reached $50 million by 1898, the Platt Amendment was inserted in the Cuban constitution to permit Washington to intervene to protect Cuban independence and "good government."[1] Sensing that the Monroe Doctrine needed updating to suit new circumstances but not wishing to affront European powers, President Theodore Roosevelt said in his message to Congress on December 6, 1904, that "chronic wrongdoing, or an impotence which results in a general loosening of the ties of civilized society" in the Caribbean or in Latin America would compel the U.S. government to employ "an international police power" to protect the Monroe Doctrine. Implicit was the message that the United States would intervene to prevent any European power from taking advantage of internal disorder to establish some form of control.[2] Roosevelt's strong words, known as the Roosevelt Corollary, opened the door to frequent twentiety-century intervention in the affairs of Caribbean and Central American states.

Intervention also came out of a strong imperialist ideology which preceded and followed Roosevelt in the administrations of McKinley, Taft, and Wilson. By the late 1800s American presidents had already sent the marines to China, Korea, Japan, Hawaii, Mexico, and Nicaragua. The year 1898 marked a war with Spain which ensured American control of the Philippines in the Pacific, and Puerto Rico and Cuba in the Caribbean. In 1903 Panama was successfully detached from Colombia to permit the construction of a canal; two years later the U.S. intervened in the Dominican Republic and in 1909 in Nicaragua. In historian Hans Schmidt's view, "The immediate objectives of American expansion were to achieve hegemony in the Caribbean and the Pacific."[3]

The opening of the Panama Canal in 1914 served further to define Caribbean sea lanes as a vital U.S. interest, especially given the German commercial interest in Haiti and elsewhere. Henceforth, the United States would always consider that it must exercise some measure of control, particularly around the Windward Channel, between Cuba and Hispaniola, through which most ships sailing to and from the canal still pass. The fact that German businessmen were numerous in Port-au-Prince and German ships frequented the Caribbean in 1914 convinced U.S. policy makers that the Kaiser's fleet might be tempted to intervene by setting up a naval base. World War I began, and although the United States was officially neutral, the possibility that German submarines might operate out of Haiti was considered a serious threat to U.S. interests generally. Haitian scholar, Suzy Castor, denies that any European power was in a position to threaten U.S. interests in the Caribbean. For her the talk of threat was a pretext while economic advantage—protection of U.S. investments, promotion of trade at the expense of the Europeans, and control of import and export tax collection—was the key reason for the occupation.[4] Although trade with the United States was increasingly important from the Haitian perspective, it represented a small percentage of U.S. commerce. Estimates of U.S. investments vary widely, but Schmidt says $4 million, minuscule compared with the $800 million in Mexico and $200 million in Cuba.[5]

Nonetheless, internal disorder, including coups d'etat and chronic violence reached new peaks in Port-au-Prince thereby creating the conditions for intervention as defined by Roosevelt. For example, in 1911, men, allegedly in the pay of local German merchants, overthrew the president. The following year an explosion in the arsenal of the presidential palace killed the newly installed head of state. In 1913 his replacement died of apparently natural causes making way for Michel Oreste, the first civilian president. A Caco uprising spelled his doom. One leader of the Cacos, Oreste Zamor (no relation), seized the presidency in Port-au-Prince while another, Davilmare Théodore, moved into Cap Haïtien. United States marines landed briefly at the Cap in response to reports of widespread looting.

After a few months as head of state Zamor was replaced by Théodore, who threatened to take the gold out of the Bank of Haiti which was controlled by a consortium of European and U.S. bankers. Faced with this threat, Roger Farnham, a vice president of the National City Bank of New York which had invested in the Bank, convinced the U.S. government to send in the marines. One of the reasons for Farnham's influence was that the Department of State had practically no competent experts on the

Caribbean.⁶ On December 17, 1914, marines landed, marched to the national bank, seized the gold, and carried it off to New York. French troops landed five months later to protect their consulate in Cap Haïtien.

General Vilbrun Guillaume Sam was then in power. In July of 1915, however, enraged relatives of persons he had ordered executed murdered him in turn. No one then seemed in charge of Haitian state affairs although life went on in the rural areas as it had done through all the years of turmoil in the capital. In Port-au-Prince cliques of elites opposed other cliques. A northern physician, Dr. Rosalvo Bobo, supported by a Caco group, was reportedly hostile to U.S. interests. The combination of all these circumstances prompted the order by the United States to move in. On the July 28, 1915, 350 white Americans landed in Port-au-Prince to begin 19 years of occupation.

Nature of the Occupation

Occupation authorities did serve the interests of one New York bank. Financier Farnham's goals were partly reached by the American presence; his bank completed its control over Haitian finances, for example. Under the occupation the U.S. authorities controlled the duties levied on imports and exports, the single largest source of government income. Such control ensured repayment of debts, but not until 1922 was the principal debt to France paid off, mainly with U.S. loans. There is much more to this period than economic interest, however. From 1915 to 1922 the U.S. military forces, which grew to approximately 2000, crushed overt resistance and consolidated their rule over 2 million Haitians. This alien white control, ending independence, brought a measure of agreement to black and brown Haitian elites.

The first step after the restoration of order in the capital was to legitimize U.S. presence because Haiti was to be nominally independent. This was done by cajoling and threatening a defiant legislature and a puppet President Sudre Dartiguenave, who finally approved a convention making Haiti a protectorate of the United States for ten years, which was later extended to 1936. With similar methods a new constitution was approved in 1918. It increased the power of the president at the expense of the legislature—thus confirming a tendency long present in Haitian politics. The 1918 constitution omitted words reserving the ownership of land to Haitian citizens which had been inserted in Dessalines' first independence constitution.

Imposition of martial law shortly after the American landing permitted speedy trials in naval courts for opponents of the new regime. When judges in the parallel civilian courts ruled in ways considered contrary to military interest, the occupation authorities succeeded in abolishing traditional lifetime judicial appointments. A revival of rural forced labor built roads but also spread rumors about the possible return of slavery. It was the reason for massive Caco revolts.

Caco revolts have been described alternatively as uprisings by hired bands or by freedom fighters and revolutionaries. Oddly, novelist Dr. Jacques Stéphen Alexis accepted both labels when he described them as "revolutionary peasants that rival factions of feudal landlords used to seize power."[7] The Cacos had no comprehensive ideology or system of beliefs regarding a new society or method of governing. Their only goals before 1915 seemed to have been the replacement of one politician by another. More important, their existence proved the Haitian countryside was largely free from the control of Port-au-Prince. This fact meant Haiti's two worlds could not be dominated by one leader before 1915.

Charlemagne Péralte changed the orientation of the Cacos and began to forge them into what could legitimately be called a liberation army. He led them in their last and possibly finest hour. A graduate of an elite secondary school in Port-au-Prince, he had been an army officer, rising to commandant in charge of the region of Léogane in 1915. From the beginning of the occupation Péralte opposed the Americans, thus obliging the president to dismiss him. He moved from Léogane to Hinche, his hometown and was imprisoned after attacking the house of the U.S. commander there.[8] Forced labor to build roads created widespread resentment, especially at Hinche, northeast of the capital, where it continued even after Port-au-Prince ordered its suspension. After his escape from prison he and Benoît Batraville organized an army here and in the north to fight forced labor and the U.S. supported government in Port-au-Prince. In Rotberg's view, from 1917 to 1919, he may have had 40,000 followers; as per Munro, he had 20,000—still a sizable force, which even dared attack Port-au-Prince.[9] Lack of weapons doomed the effort. By the time Péralte was surprised and shot to death in his own camp by a U.S. marine, possibly 2,000 Haitians had died as the occupation forces systematically crushed all forms of Caco resistance.[10] As a result, by the end of 1920 the traditional threat of rural-based movements against governments in Port-au-Prince had ceased. Jean Dominique reports seeing a representation of Péralte as a loa in a rural Vodoo temple, but the memory of Péralte did not become the consistent, powerful symbol that General Sandino's name became in Nicaragua for his resistance to U.S. occupation. The reason may be, as Castor suggests, that like other Caco groups the movement of Péralte had no general economic and social program which could appeal to the masses then or now. Roger Gaillard's recent volumes on the American occupation should increase the interest in Péralte among students and others, however.[11]

News of forced labor, the revolt, and general administrative problems plaguing the occupation force reached Washington. After hearings in the Senate a decision was made to reorganize the administration to ensure a clear chain of command, good communication, and centralized control so that marines or others in some isolated community such as Hinche could not make their own policy. From 1922 to 1929 the newly appointed high commissioner, Brigadier General John Russell, headed the combined military and civilian structure, and the legislature elected Louis Borno president in April 1922.

Attempts were made to change the economy, making it more efficient, productive and, of course, integrating it more effectively into the world capitalist system. For example, aerial surveys were supposed to help consolidate land holdings for a more efficient agriculture, in decline since the land reforms introduced by Pétion broke up most large estates. Some U.S. companies took advantage of the changes in the constitution permitting foreign ownership of land, and U.S. investments increased three-fold from $4 million in 1915 to $14 million in 1930.[12] Most agricultural operations by the United States were not successful: "By 1930 American companies owned only 5,291 hectares in Haiti, of which the sugar company [Hasco] had 3,034. 14,479 hectares were leased, mostly from private Haitian owners. The total was less than two percent of the estimated amount of land in the Haitian plains where most of the country's arable land was situated."[13] Purchasing or leasing of land from the government, the largest landholder still, often had the severely negative effect of forcing the eviction of peasants who believed they owned the land, however. The Haitian American Sugar Company (HASCO) built a large sugar mill which is still the most significant industrial enterprise in the republic.

Americans created a Service Technique which opened agricultural vocational schools and set up demonstration farms in an effort to diversify agriculture. Under U.S. direction, government expenditures devoted to agriculture increased from 1 percent of all expenditures in 1923–24 to 10 percent in 1928–29. In addition to schools and farms, this money went to pay for rural health clinics, extension agents, and road improvements.[14] Americans introduced an automatic telephone system in urban areas, dredged harbors, and constructed bridges. For the first time in Haitian history Port-au-Prince was linked with Cap Haïtien by road. The value of Haitian money was stabilized by linking it with the U.S. dollar. The marines trained a new and professional army called the Garde d'Haïti. The first significant public health measures were taken.

Because the U.S. authorities controlled the collection of customs, the major source of income, they could decide budget priorities. For them the most important expenditure was the servicing of the external debt, owed to the United States after 1922. By 1927, 40 percent of the Haitian budget was spent on debt repayment.[15] The peasant coffee growers, whose crop was and is heavily taxed, contributed the most.

A keenly felt negative feature of the occupation reshaped Haitian self-identity in the first world of urban elites briefly and temporarily drawing them closer to each other and some even to the rural world. At the start of the occupation many brown and tan mulattoes who monopolized high positions had expected to collaborate as equals with the Americans. Several had been educated in France and considered themselves as the cultivated equal of any white person. Although the head of the initial invasion force, Admiral Caperton, had set a good example by fraternizing with these elites and by showing respect for the people he met, his successors and the low ranking military men offended the established elite and the masses. The completely white and mainly southern U.S. service personnel discriminated against Haitians without distinction as to color or class. For the most part, they refused to learn French, kept nonetheless as the official language. They kept to themselves in social clubs, particularly after the arrival of white women. According to Schmidt, "effective racial segregation became firmly established as an important facet of the occupation."[16] Stéphen Alexis provided urban Haitian readers with an image of that racism in his 1933 novel, *Le nègre masqué*. He draws a sharp picture of the fury of the white American Seaton against the Haitian mulatto Roger Sinclair who dared love a white woman. The somewhat unrealistic ending also shows how the U.S. occupation encouraged a slight nostalgia for France. In general, Americans showed utter disregard for the pride of the elites. Professing cultural and racial superiority, the Americans sought to impose their values. Black and brown elites and many peasants shared grievances, at least for some years.

Americans also misused the very institutions they had imposed a decade earlier. Thus, the anticipated elections for 1930 were cancelled, protesting journalists found themselves behind bars, and taxes were raised. Raymond Leslie Buell, an expert on U.S. imperialism, pointed out in 1929 that Hatians had less freedom than Puerto Ricans and Filipinos who were not even nominally independent.[17] In October 1929 the situation worsened when students in the vocational schools, already unhappy about some educational policies, went on strike. In December a strike by customs employees sparked a more general uprising, and in a confused confrontation with 1500 peasants who had marched to Les Cayes town, marines killed at least a dozen Haitians.

Washington reacted to the disorder and rebellion by sending another commission to investigate. All U.S. presidents since Woodrow Wilson had expressed their doubts about the occupation, and the commission provided an opportunity to initiate its end. Borno was told not to expect further support for his reelection, and promotion of Haitians to important positions in the military was promised. In October 1930 a new legislature was installed, and the following month its members elected Sténio Vincent president. Vincent, like his two predecessors under American occupation, was a mulatto. A civilian U.S. minister replaced General Russell who departed. The process of American withdrawal had begun.

Each year after 1930 urban elite Haitians took more power back into their own hands. In 1931 they took over the Public Works Department, for example. Fair-skinned men tended to move into these administrative posts while black men, who moved into the officer corps of the Garde d'Haïti, found that their training and promotion conferred elite status. After a visit by President Franklin D. Roosevelt, the only American head of state ever to visit Haiti, the military left on August 21, 1934, two years ahead of schedule. This gesture was a sign of FDR's new approach to the Caribbean and Latin America. American civilian officials also departed except for financial advisors who ensured enough control over the national bank that Haiti would continue repayment of debts, which amounted to $11 million in 1934. Although direct political control ended, for the next 13 years U.S. influence in the bank meant that economically Haiti was not fully sovereign. Faithfully, Haiti repaid its dept.

Occupation Impact: Direct and Indirect

It is generally agreed that the American reforms had few lasting direct effects of any kind, good or bad, for nineteen years was too short a time; goals were unclear and inconsistent except for ensuring that no other power would intervene; linguistic differences and race prejudice limited communication; no significant sustained externally financed aid program was tried; and American techniques of rule contradicted expressed U.S. desires for stability, respect for law, and institutionalization.

It is true that the U.S. forces created new institutions such as a unified, professional, and modern army, the Garde d'Haïti, which had 4,000 men by 1934, but this force was soon to be manipulated and subjugated to the will of a few ambitious leaders. The vocational schools, modeled on Tuskegee Institute, could have been an important institutional contribution, but they were marred by a colonial style arrogance and a tendency to pit them against the traditional schools. The latter, the intellectually oriented French-style school system, which Haitians valued, had suffered from lack of funds during the occupation sparking resentment against vocational education.

Urban Haitians tended to perceive Americans as racists and self-serving exploiters who used Haitian institutions and the gun for their own advantage, not the Haitians' advantage. Therefore, it is not surprising they rejected American innovations once the marines left.

What did last was the definitive centralization of power in Port-au-Prince after the suppression of Caco resistance, the construction of roads, and the strengthening of administrative control. No matter how one may view the Cacos—as mercenaries or patriots—they disappeared during the U.S. occupation and henceforth no Haitian government needed to fear regional peasant uprisings. Rural ports such as St. Marc, Jérémie, and Jacmel were further undermined by the roads which diminished the importance of coastal shipping and by a differential customs policy making trade through Port-au-Prince cheaper than elsewhere. More than ever before, the rural areas became politically and economically insignificant. Who ruled Port-au-Prince ruled Haiti, and postoccupation leaders reaped the benefits.

Another permanent result of U.S. occupation was the institutionalization of economic and commercial ties between Haiti and the United States, both at the governmental and the nongovernmental level. German business and banking interests were expelled, and the French banking and business interests faded. Haiti also entered the dollar zone where it has remained. The value of the Haitian currency or *gourde* is fixed in terms of American currency, and both monies circulate as legal tender.

The U.S. occupation also facilitated the emigration of Haitian migrant labor to take part in the sugar booms of Cuba and the Dominican Republic. For instance, Haitian emigration to Cuba increased from 1,512 in 1913 to an average of more than 16,000 per year during the 1920s.[18] The Americans promoted transport and encouraged the sugar companies to recruit in Haiti. While U.S. capital invested in Cuban sugar totalled $600 million by 1929, the principal beneficiaries of cheap and industrious Haitian labor were locally owned Cuban and Dominican estates. During the Great Depression hundreds of thousands of Haitian migrants were forcibly repatriated from both countries as King Sugar declined.

The occupation also brought about long term if erratic links between the U.S. military and some Haitians. U.S. marines trained the first professional military in Haitian history and retained formal and informal contacts after 1934. The Haitian Army, but not the various paraprofessional forces, continued to look to the U.S. for training, equipment, and tactical doctrines such as counterinsurgency.

During World War II Haiti declared war on the side of the Allies but committed no forces, offering only onshore facilities. U.S. coast guardsmen were stationed in Haiti, and some ties resumed with the politically fragmented army.

After World War II formal and informal military ties warmed, especially under President Magloire, an ex-officer trained by the Americans. In 1959 President François Duvalier requested and received a U.S. military mission to train his army. However, he was soon to expel this mission whose work had been undermined by Duvalier's political purges of army officers.

Jean-Claude Duvalier also turned to the U.S. shortly after taking office in 1971 to train an elite military unit called the Leopards. During the Carter administration all formal military ties were broken, but they have been resumed with a very modest U.S. Coast Guard involvement in the training of the tiny Haitian navy. This training is an outcome of the agreement whereby the Haitian government authorizes the Coast Guard to patrol Haitian waters to deter illegal immigration.

INTELLECTUAL RENAISSANCE

A third and most unexpected longterm consequence of American occupation was the intellectual renaissance experienced by both black and mulatto educated elites. One stream of thought paralleled and contributed to the Negritude movement emerging in Africa, France, and the West Indies as well as the Pan African movement in North America, London, and the English-speaking countries of the Caribbean and Africa. Another stream, inspired by the Russian Revolution of 1917, spawned a tiny Haitian Communist Party and intense speculation about the advantages and disadvantages of socialism and communism.

The desire and the ability to articulate changing social, economic, and political concerns in the form of poetry and prose are very strong in Haitian intellectual history. There is an urge to write that is pervasive in the educational system beginning at least at the high school level, among teachers and students. Among the masses the urge translates itself into oral forms such as songs, stories, and aphorisms which are constantly changing. These are reasons Haitian literature, including that of the Haitian diaspora, is probably the most dynamic and self-searching in the Caribbean.

In a recent book on Negritude poets in French, Ellen Kennedy, who knows very well the full range of poetry in French, included seven Haitians out of a total of 13 Caribbean poets. No other country—in Africa or elsewhere—could equal the Haitian contribution to this intellectual movement even though none of the men credited with founding the movement came from Haiti.[19] Authors of an encyclopedia of Caribbean writers—English-, Spanish-, and French-speaking—found the most authors in Haiti, even more than in Cuba which has double the Haitian population, a much higher per capita income, and over 90 percent literacy compared with probably 20 percent literacy in Haiti.[20] Blocked politically by the white foreigners; aware of the weaknesses of Haitian institutions and the corruption of the past; fearful of continuing isolation, yet proud of Haitian qualities; searching for new ideologies and forms of organization; newly inspired by the culture of the masses, Haitians began to write and publish a new generation of well crafted plays, novels, songs, and poetry.

Literacy and discussion societies flourished while reviews and journals, political organizations and clubs drew inspiration from the intellectuals. The mulatto elite was reinforced, and a small black elite grew in numbers as land-owning blacks migrated to Port-au-Prince, went to school, and became professionals and business people. Dr. Jean Price-Mars was a key figure in setting the agenda for discussion about Haitian identity, culture, and goals. His interests went far beyond a recognition of the African heritage and the importance of peasant life. He condemned the exploitation of women, and he called for the reorganization of the educational system to fit the environment and the real needs of the people.[21]

In his *Vocation* book Price-Mars took a more political stand: Haiti needs to create a "national thought" or a unifying ideology. Charlemagne Péralte's crusade must be seen as heroic resistance and might be a part of that national thought, he wrote.[22] Facing squarely the issue of mulatto versus black, Price-Mars denied that the motive force of Haitian political history was the struggle between two castes based on color. Rather, he saw Haitian political history as dominated by the struggle between cliques of blacks and mulattoes who belonged—both of them—to one dominant class.

Although the brown-skinned people outnumbered the blacks within the highest political and economic strata between independence and 1915, blacks such as Salomon and Soulouque had been president. In his view, black rulers were as guilty as the mulattoes: they all ignored the masses' best interests no matter what their color. Price-Mars was no Marxist, but he recognized the power of class interest as one important explanation for human behavior. He reiterated this view again at the end of his life in a debate with René Piquion, black writer and journalist, who claimed that color was the key to Haiti. Price-Mars wrote in an open letter to Piquion that "here as elsewhere the 'social issue' is the opposition which raises up the disinherited, the 'proletarians'—of whatever color they may be— against those—of whatever color they may be—who are rich and who exploit them by profiting exhorbitantly from their work."[23]

This black intellectual's long life from 1876 to 1969, extensive literary output, correspondence with Caribbeans, French intellectuals, and politicians, American blacks, and later with Africans gave him considerable authority within his country and within the black world. The shock of the occupation inspired him to ask the most basic questions about himself and the failures of Haitian history.

His young compatriots began *La Nouvelle Ronde* review and explicitly repudiated foreign, mainly French, models and styles which had dominated nineteenth-century Haitian literature. They also rejected the idea of art for art's sake and an apolitical literature represented by the contributions to the original *La Ronde* review. Others such as Emile Roumer, Philippe Thoby-Marcelin, and Carl Brouard founded and wrote for *La Revue Indigène* in 1927. Some of these writers were urban and fair in color, but they were dedicated to black culture, peasant life, and African origins. Some black and brown intellectuals began meeting in the late 1930s in a group they called Les Griots (troubadors or storytellers in Africa). They were most interested in African origins, "racial authenticity," and "racial determinism." They exhibited anti-white and anti-mulatto feelings; and they used their writing to praise the black rulers of the past. In 1938 this group, which included the physician Dr. François Duvalier, began to publish a journal called *Les Griots*.

The Griots believed that color, rather than class, was the key to understanding Haitian history. The struggle for preeminence between black and mulatto was the motive force of Haitian history. They also looked outside Haiti to other blacks; thus they felt strong bonds of kinship with Ethiopia which had just been invaded by Mussolini. They believed the future belonged to them if they could organize against their enemies. J. Michael

Dash calls them narcissistic and paranoid, but they also were working to legitimize black rule.[24]

Both mulattoes and blacks, middle class and poor, began to dip into the well of rural Haiti for anthropological studies and for literary inspiration thus participating in what is called *Indigénisme.* Some also saw Haiti's destiny linked with revolutionary forces in the outside world; in 1934 Jacques Roumain, then 27 years old, founded the Haitian Communist Party. In opposition stood the venerable Dantès Bellegarde who had headed the Department of Education and wrote extensively about Haitian history. He continued to believe that French culture was the foundation of Haitian culture with the French language and the Roman Catholic religion. Haitian culture was an extension of metropolitan French culture, in his view.

Thus, a productive debate over the definition of Haitian culture, the ties with France, the African heritage, and the possibilities of democratic or Marxian socialism began under the eyes of the American military and continued into the two decades between the occupation and the Duvalier family domination. The debate and the literary output confirmed Haiti's literary independence from France. The founding of the Bureau d'Ethnologie by Jacques Roumain in 1941 also provided a scientific basis for the study of Haitian life and culture.[25]

INTERIM 1934–1957

This unifying race consciousness, reborn during Haiti's second colonial experience, remained strong during the post-occupational period 1934–1957, but the old divisive color distinctions between black elite and mulatto elite also reemerged. An essential difference from the pre-occupation period was that the black middle class had grown, and with their increased numbers they were in a better position to struggle for the power, wealth, prestige which control of the state gave.

The policies of two fair-skinned presidents from 1930 to 1946 prepared the way for a strong black reaction. Many blacks perceived both Sténio Vincent and Elie Lescot as antiblack and as disdainful of the peasant components of the national culture. President Vincent had led the country to its second independence on August 21, 1934, but he antagonized blacks by quickly concentrating extensive powers in his own hands, providing for his reelection despite constitutional restrictions, and limiting freedom of speech.

For his personal protection he built up a select 500 man presidential guard separate from the army.[26] The army left by the Americans was dominated by highly professional black officers headed by Colonel D.P. Calixte. There was bound to be some tension between the guard and the army and between civilian and military due to color and competition for control and influence. Vincent feared the U.S. trained military and the precedent of other countries where U.S. intervention had been followed by military rule as in the Dominican Republic and Nicaragua. In the Dominican Republic Rafael Trujillo, who had the same position as Colonel Calixte, staged a coup in 1930.

And then there was Haitian history itself, dominated as it was by military leaders. Thus, after a confusing incident during which an officer of the presidential guard was shot, Calixte was blamed. Some mulattoes believed this was the beginning of his bid for power. In January 1938 the president, reacting to these events, dismissed the head of the army and began a purge of black officers. In exile Calixte claimed he was the victim of political intrigues.[27] President Vincent had already been taking other precautions to avoid the fate of his civilian colleagues elsewhere in the Caribbean by practically disarming the army. Most weapons were transported to the presidential palace, an old Haitian custom to be employed twenty years later by President François Duvalier.

A stripped military may have been one reason the army had earlier failed to protect Haitian workers in October 1937 in the Dominican Republic. That month Dominican military and civilians murdered almost 20,000 black men, women, and children in order to "whiten" their country by killing and driving out recent and longtime black residents labelled "Haitian." Perhaps they also wished to take some belated revenge for the twenty-year Haitian occupation which Dominicans still resent. Even though there were Haitian soldiers on the frontier, and they knew about the bloodshed nearby, they did nothing.

There was no doubt about Dominican culpability, and Trujillo promised to pay an indemnity of $750,000, a derisory sum, but there is no record the whole amount was paid. Nor is it clear who received whatever was paid.[28] The mild response of President Vincent to this shocking event must have contributed to his own reputation as antiblack. It also suggests he pocketed the money.

In 1941 American officials intervened quietly in Haitian politics to prevent Sténio Vincent from serving a third term. He agreed to withdraw, and the legislature elected Elie Lescot, a man with very close ties to Trujillo and the United States. The new president did little to endear himself to blacks or nationalists as he received money from Trujillo and extended the "jurisdiction of military courts to all offenses and persons."[29] These were the same tribunals which had been set up during the American occupation.

In a direct confrontation with a rising black consciousness, President Lescot led a campaign against Voodoo and preferred appointing mulattoes rather than blacks to high positions. In an effort to draw Haiti even closer to the United States, he proposed that American priests replace the French clergy who dominated the Catholic church and schools. Demonstrating his sympathies Lescot declared war on Japan one day after the United States, and in return Washington pledged to purchase Haitian cotton. Under the provisions of Lend Lease, Haiti received weapons and tanks. A detachment of the U.S. Coast Guard was stationed at Bizoton just outside Port-au-Prince and Lescot offered the famous Môle St. Nicolas to the U.S. as a base.[30] In 1944 Reynolds Aluminum was granted permission to mine bauxite in Grand'Anse Department halfway between Port-au-Prince and Les Cayes.[31]

Like his predecessors, Lescot would not willingly give up power at the end of his term of office, no matter what the law and constitution stated. In 1945 he began attempts to change the constitution so that he could succeed himself. His antiblack reputation plus his anticonstitutional gestures sparked strikes in Port-au-Prince. Intellectual ferment also grew in the urban areas. Political ideas along a broad spectrum poured from the elites. Newspapers, discussion groups, public speeches, meetings, and alliances reveled in a grand debate about the future of the republic. New waves of black migrants to Port-au-Prince nourished a growing working class constituency, and men such as the populist leader Daniel Fignolé tried to organize them into the Worker-Peasant Movement (MOP). Radicals formed the Haitian Revolutionary Front.

In a similar situation before 1915 this would have been the moment for a Caco uprising from the north to remove Lescot, but this time the military in Port-au-Prince intervened, taking over the government. Lescot went into exile thus preparing the way for new presidential elections which would give black intellectuals and the middle class their day. The close of World War II saw Haiti alive with long frustrated hopes and expectations.

Out of eight candidates for president in 1946, seven were identified as black. On August 16, 1945, the National Assembly elected Dumarsais Estimé. Shortly after taking office, Estimé, a black man who had studied under Price-Mars and then had taught in the Lycée Pétion, began taking measures which provided opportunities for black elites and which showed his respect for Haitian cultural tradition. He used Voodoo on official occasions the way Catholic symbols and priests had been used in the past. He introduced an income tax, promoted rural cooperatives and model farms, and expressed opposition to foreign ownership of land without, however, prohibiting it in his own constitution of November 22, 1946. He nationalized the banana industry, which had been owned by the American Standard Fruit Company, by putting it in the hands of black landholders and business people who were politically allied with him, but this action contributed to the industry's demise. In what later proved to have been a significant act, the president promoted many blacks in the civil service and into the cabinet including his former student Dr. François Duvalier. The latter, who had also been secretary general of Fignolé's party, the Worker-Peasant Movement (MOP), was appointed minister of labor.

The Estimé presidency from 1946 to 1950 witnessed a period of creative exuberance in the plastic arts, though somewhat different from the literary outpouring of the 1920s and 1930s. An American, Dewitt Peters, had founded the Centre d'Art in Port-au-Prince to encourage Haitian painters and sculptors. In small towns and rural areas he found much talent, particularly among Voodoo priests. Another American, Seldon Rodman, joined these efforts, and Haitian art, labeled primitive because of its simple and direct realism, folk subjects, and unmixed colors, quickly gained renown.

As Estimé's term of office began to approach its stipulated end, he, like his predecessor, alienated himself from most Haitians by trying to alter the constitution to permit his re-election by forcing workers to purchase government bonds and favoring small groups of friends with the advantages of office and government contracts. The military was ready to try its hand at ruling, and the mulattoes were anxious to promote a man closer to their interests. On May 10, 1950, soldiers, headed by Colonel Paul Magloire, a black man backed by the malattoes, forced Estimé to resign. Despite this humiliating political finish, President Estimé had succeeded in encouraging many young middle-class blacks in urban areas to aspire to high office.[32] After a few years of military rule, and after the death of Estimé, they would try their chances again.

That October Paul Magloire won the election for president, a milestone because it marked the first time people voted directly for their head of state. Previously the legislature had this responsibility. Like Estimé, Magloire was phenotypically black, but people perceived him to be more responsive to brown-skin elite interests. The pattern of his appointments of high ranking officials and his favoritism toward businesses owned by mulattoes proved this orientation. In other words, he was a "front man", and the

Haitians invented a long time ago a word for this political style, to wit, *la politique de doublure* (two-faced politics). In historian Nicholls's words, "The regime of Magloire represents the last successful attempt by the old elite to reassert its political preeminence behind the mask of the black colonel."[33]

Like Lescot, President Magloire cultivated carefully his ties with Washington, and he won the confidence of Americans interested in Haiti. Charming, gregarious, and self-confident, he was able to exert some influence over Americans and Haitians even while in exile in the U.S. He encouraged close ties with other countries in the Caribbean and visited the United States. Richard Nixon, then Vice President, visited Haiti in turn. During Magloire's presidency U.S. and United Nations programs contributed to the beginning of a dam on the Artibonite River and the expansion of tourism. Until a disastrous hurricane battered the island in 1954 the economy, as viewed from Port-au-Prince, prospered. What was less visible was the dramatic increase in the public debt as funds disappeared from the public treasury. The urban elite enjoyed these years.[34]

As Magloire's six-year term approached its prescribed close, rumors spread in Port-au-Prince that he wished to succeed himself which was against the constitution then in force. Demonstrations and bombings forced Magloire to resign at the end of 1956. But, by ceding power to his comrades in the army over whom he had considerable influence, he was obviously maneuvering to hold on to power. Not unexpectedly, the army proposed installing him at the head of a military regime, but more demonstrations in the capital dashed his hopes. Observers report that the union of truck, bus, and taxi drivers, led by Dr. François Duvalier, was particularly active in the demonstrations. Magloire gave up and went into comfortable exile in the United States where tens of thousands of his compatriots would join him in the next few years.

A series of interim presidents took office before the elections scheduled for September 22, 1957. As the elections approached François Duvalier and Louis Dejoie, a brown-skinned industrialist, emerged as favorites. Duvalier had important worker connections through the Mouvement Ouvrier-Paysan (MOP) of which he was the secretary, and his association with the late President Estimé had not tainted him with corruption. He had been associated with the intellectual movements affirming the cultural identity of Haiti although some might have believed him a racist. He had had close association with Americans working in public health programs and knew many people in his capacity as physician. Duvalier had some but not complete American backing[35] and, more important, the leaders of the army supported him. Dejoie was popular in the south where he built a large business. After the departure of Magloire, Colonel Antonio Kébreau, a friend of Duvalier, emerged as the military commander.

During the voting itself soldiers were stationed at polling places ostensibly to ensure a peaceful election. Naturally, Duvalier's opponents claimed the army influenced the results, but this is not certain. In any case, on September 22, 1957, Duvalier won a six-year term of office, and his followers won a majority of seats in the new legislature. Among those followers were the partisans of former President Estimé, blacks, urban workers, and particularly the truck and taxi drivers. Women also voted for the first time. On October 22, 1957, Duvalier took office as head of state at the age of 50.

Francois Duvailer 1957–1971

Haiti's newest president seemed a promising representative of the growing black bourgeoisie of professionals, civil servants, and rural landholders. His father, who had been a teacher, journalist, and justice of the peace, was firmly anchored in the lower middle class. Hoping for something better for his son, he sent him to the Lycée Pétion, a bastion of the middle classes and those aspiring to middle-class status who could not afford the Catholic schools or institutions abroad. There he met and studied under future president Estimé. He also met and knew Price-Mars either at the lycée or in Port-au-Prince intellectual circles. Like Price-Mars, he attended medical school, but, reflecting the newer political and economic orientation of Haiti, continued his public health education in America, not France, in the 1940s. He married a nurse, Simone Ovide.

Intellectually, he allied himself early with the black ideologists in Port-au-Prince, praising the black African tradition and the unique blend of cultures in Haiti in his articles and books. In 1934 he wrote with his friend Lorimer Denis, *Les tendances d'une génération;* in 1948; *Le problème des classes à traverse l'histoire d'Haïti.* In 1949 he published *L'avenir du pays et l'action néfaste de M. Foisset.* He also prepared several medical articles particularly about yaws and other diseases in the republic.

The 128-page book, *Problème des classes à travers l'histoire d'Haïti,* which is currently sold by the government printing office, is a clear expression of Duvalier's black power ideas. It was a warning about what he might do published nine years before he took office in 1957. For Duvalier "class" is a group of people who primarily share a way of thinking, feeling, and acting; it is "a collective personality."[36] In Haiti there have been two classes ever since colonial days: first the freed and the slaves, then, after independence to the present (1948), the mulattoes and the blacks. Freedmen and women felt superior to slaves prior to 1804, and blacks were still pariahs.[37]

Duvalier complained in this book that all the great leaders of Haiti have been black, Toussaint, Dessalines, Lysius Salomon, Antoine Simon, and beginning in 1946 Dumarsais Estimé, his friend. Under the mulatto leaders the black middle classes, and his own generation in particular, suffered most; "From our most tender childhood years we knew deprivation because we belonged to the brave middle class which, according to J.C. Dorsainvil, was the most cruelly struck by misery."[38] By "misery" Duvalier explained that educational and job opportunities were denied the blacks while mulattoes who went abroad for their education returned to fill the most prestigious positions. Some middle-class blacks educated in Haiti went mad. "But," he warns his compatriots, "the Great Reparation must soon begin." ("Mais la Grande Réparation devait bientôt commencer.")[39] The leadership of Estimé will change Haiti, but Duvalier warns that blacks may betray their fellow blacks by conniving with the enemy, letting the mulattoes rule through a black; and because of personal weaknesses which he enumerates meticulously. He complains that blacks betray each other; they are egocentric; they are too egalitarian "which destroys the principle of hierarchy and respect for traditions."[40] Therefore, blacks cannot put all the blame for their condition on the mulattoes, and one mulatto president, Geffrard, tried to establish an "equilibrium" between black elites and mulatto elites in terms of access of wealth, power, and prestige.

Dr. Duvalier and Lorimer Denis conclude their book with an appeal to Haitian elites to study the color issue in Haiti and to try to unite. They must also study their national traditions just as the Turks under the leadership of Ataturk, a man Duvalier admired, studied their past.

In short, Dr. Duvalier was an articulate thinking member of an intellectual school which was both race and class conscious, resentful about mulatto control, and critical of perceived black weaknesses. Like Turkey, Haiti needed a strong ruler who could overcome past injustice, black inabilities, and mulatto arrogance. For Duvalier color was the key to understanding Haitian history, and once he took power he drew around himself a group of black intellectuals with similar feelings.

Duvalier's fourteen year rule of Haiti was the longest since Jean-Pierre Boyer in the early nineteenth century. For the first half of these years, Duvalier eliminated competition or potential competition and consolidated his power as no one else had ever done. A state of siege prevailed because of a vigorous opposition movement, and Duvalier fanned the flames by terrorizing the population. The defeated candidates and elements in the military wished to remove him, he correctly believed. In 1958 and 1959 two limited invasions of the island threatened him; the first may have been part of an abortive military coup, and the second was Cuba-supported. U.S. marines, who had been invited to the country in January 1959 to train soldiers, apparently helped repel the small force.[41]

In 1961 a group of young men, including the brilliant novelist and physician Jacques-Stéphen Alexis, invaded the island in another effort to overthrow the president, but they were captured and killed. Other landings and small uprisings took place in 1964, 1967, 1968, and 1970. Duvalier repelled them all by tactics making him the all powerful, absolute ruler of the country.

One of the first tactics was to destroy the military as an independent force. Thus, he removed the very officers whose friendship had assisted him win the election. Following the example of President-Emperor Faustin Soulouque, he created his own militia, nicknamed the tontons macoutes or bogeymen in 1959. Three years later he built it into what is now officially called the Volontaires de la Sécurité Nationale (VSN) or National Security Volunteers, whose members were and are allegedly recruited from taxi drivers, the unemployed, criminal elements, as well as from Voodoo priests and priestesses, and others. The VSN, like civil servants, pledged their allegiance to the president who soon took to calling himself the incarnation of Haiti. He was also careful enough to prevent anyone from rising within the VSN to challenge him and therefore unhesitatingly removed its first leader who, like Colonel Kébreau, had supported Duvalier when he needed it most.

Unlike most of his predecessors—except Estimé—Duvalier wished to establish lines of communucation with Haiti's second rural world outside the administrative and political channels already in existence. He had already shown his respect for Voodoo and won over some of its priests and priestesses by threats, rewards, and his own knowledge of the sacred. He promoted the interests of the rural-based bilingual (and potential middle class) black middlemen purchasing coffee from the peasants and selling it to the white and mulatto-owned export houses in Port-au-Prince. He protected the interests of the rural black middlewoman, the "Madan Saras," and the women retailers purchasing rice and other food crops for sale in the capital. One way he did so was by forbidding the exporters to purchase coffee directly from peasant producers and by licensing middlemen.[42] To circumvent the mulattoes, who controlled medium and large businesses and who opposed Duvalier, the president won the allegiance of smaller traders of Lebanese and Syrian origin who always felt somewhat insecure without political allies. He appointed one of their number mayor of the capital and probably recruited some into the tontons macoutes operating in Port-au-Prince where the Arabs are concentrated. Some Madan Saras and coffee middlemen also joined the VSN.

All these business people regularly contributed funds for nonexistent charities or projects launched by the head of state, or by his wife, who also began to play a significant role in Haitian politics. Hasco, Reynolds Aluminum, and other companies reportedly paid their taxes in advance when the government found itself short of cash. Following another Haitian tradition, excise taxes paid on cement, tobacco, and several other basic items did not go to the treasury but, rather, to a parallel institution, the Régie du Tabac or Tobacco Office, used by the Duvalier family as a personal treasury.

Some of this money paid the police and the military. Once they were tamed, they were given the task of keeping the family in power. It has been estimated by several sources that about 30 percent of the annual budget went to maintain the "forces of order," but still less than the 65 percent spent on military and police in 1848 under Soulouque.[43]

Having monopolized the forces of coercion and liquidated the above ground opposition, President Duvalier set about to coopt the Catholic and Anglican churches. He expelled foreign clergy and secured their replacement by black Haitians acceptable to him. The threat of loss of funds, expulsion, and harassment converted the churches, after a brief struggle, into grudging accomplices of the regime.

Little that Duvalier did to consolidate power was new to Haitian history, but he cumulated the most brutal methods of the past while shrewdly benefiting from the changes brought about by the U.S. occupation. As long as he could control Port-au-Prince and play on black ideology he could control the country, for the peasants were cynical about all politicians, preferring to avoid contact with central authorities and its local representatives.

After the legislative elections of 1961 Duvalier claimed that he had just been reelected to another six-year term even though no notice had been given and even though his mandate would not end until 1963. His bizarre claim was based on the fact that his name did appear as a heading to the ballots used for the national assembly elections. To spare himself the trouble again, Duvalier changed the constitution in 1964 to permit his election as president for life, and on June 14 of the same year the voters confirmed this new office. Like his other techniques, this was not new. Pétion had been declared president for life at the beginning of Haitian independence. The new 1964 constitution also changed the flag from blue and red to black and red, a symbol of the triumph of blacks.

After 1964 President Duvalier seemed more secure, although he continued to spend large sums of money on security. In Nicholls's view, Duvalier believed that once he was secure he could complete the modernization of a truly black nation which he believed Estimé had begun.[44]

Although in their writings Duvalier and Lorimer Denis had called for educational reforms including the extensive use of Creole in schools, plus economic reforms for the benefit of the workers and peasants, he did nothing to improve the lowest classes' material well-being, and generally ignored the Creole-speaking rural areas except for some adult literacy programs. He was afraid that any reforms would weaken his hold on the people, and in his paranoia feared retribution from people he had oppressed. He politicized the educational system. Loyalists found it easier to gain admission to the university and win fellowships which were in part payment for reports on the politics of other students.[45]

Duvalier as president was able to consolidate control of both internal events and contacts with the external world in the presidential palace. The effects were disastrous for smaller cities and towns which incurred presidential disfavor. For instance, the coffee port of Jacmel with its brown elites had staunchly opposed Duvalier in the 1957 election. Its port was stripped of its coffee export rights, and the road to the capital was allowed to deteriorate to a rough track. The stifling of local initiative caused total agricultural production to decline, withering government revenues. Duvalier responded with systematic neglect and indifference, siphoning off funds for security, and leaving the rural areas and the rest of the country to rot.

Duvalier initially pursued a pro-American foreign policy which resulted in increased U.S. aid, prompted in part by the proximity of Castro's Cuba. The corruption, brutality, and venality of the Duvalier administration resulted in the Kennedy administration terminating most military and technical aid programs in August 1962. A few activities were resumed under President Lyndon B. Johnson, but major foreign aid did not return until the 1970s.

External isolation was one of Duvalier's trump cards. Although the economy depended on coffee exports, Duvalier and no one else controlled the strings used to coopt and to coerce. If foreign aid was not available on his terms, the president could refuse it. In retrospect Dr. Duvalier seems among the most bizarre and ruthless presidents of a country known for its erratic leaders. Conspiratorial, racist, paranoiac and reportedly drawn to the dark side of Voodoo, Duvalier was a master of political cunning and manipulation. Estimates of the numbers of Haitians who died for their opposition or alleged opposition to Duvalier range from 30,000 to 60,000.

JEAN-CLAUDE DUVALIER, 1971—

Realizing he was mortally ill, Duvalier manipulated the constitution to introduce a hereditary presidency. Christophe and Soulouque had tried to create hereditary monarchies. After the death of the father on April 14, 1971, the only son, Jean-Claude, then nineteen years old, took power and began to rule, first with the assistance of his mother, Simone Ovide Duvalier, and after his marriage in 1980, with the aid of his wife Michele Bennett, scion of a newly wealthy mulatto family.

The first decade of the new president for life began with visible political and economic liberalization. The young man brought in some new faces and invited technocrats to return home to participate in the "economic revolution" called *jean-claudisme* which he said he had launched.[36]

Attracted by the promise of a pragmatic emphasis on development, many Haitians did return home, and discussions about the future political evolution of the country became much freer. Economist Jean-Jacques Honorat published in Haiti his *Enquête sur le développement,* a daring criticism of past elites, which raised many questions about the country among intellectuals in Haiti and abroad.[47] Honorat, who associated himself with the black or "Noiriste" tradition of Estimé and Duvalier, could nonetheless criticize both black and brown elites for their selfish oppression of the masses who have become passive and suspicious. He praised Voodoo as authentically Haitian and as a means peasants use against rapacious elites and foreign interests.[48] In another daring gesture, Grégoire Eugène, Professor of Constitutional and Civil Law at the State University, called for new political parties.

Gradually under its new president Haiti began to reduce its severe isolation and to explore new avenues. Educational specialists from several countries joined Haitians in examining a decrepit system which failed to serve most Haitians. Lacking any significant trade agreements, Haiti began to talk to its Dominican and other Caribbean neighbors. Its extreme poverty made its market unattractive and its gesture in 1974 toward possible membership in CARICOM, the Caribbean Community, was rebuffed.

Decades of agricultural neglect were beginning to be redressed by French, Canadian, West German, U.S., and Israeli projects, as well as those of private voluntary organizations whose efforts were made more welcome. Road construction and maintenance were initiated, especially to Jacmel, Les Cayes, Cap Haïtien, and other departmental centers. Haitian urban wages, among the lowest in the world, were used to attract industries to assemble components for export. By the end of the 1970s, over 200 such plants had opened employing 40,000 persons, mostly women, in the capital. These signs of economic renewal were dealt a major blow though by the post-1973 eruption of international energy prices, with Haiti totally dependent on imported fuel. Nor was the Haitian government with its conservative foreign policy and internal repression a likely candidate for oil-exporters' aid.

Politically the new regime showed signs of relying more on cooption and less on coercion than its predecessor. The widow Duvalier's influence waned while that of the more worldly wife of Jean-Claude grew. The ability of the regime to win the support of some technocrats, local businessmen, and foreign aid officials were considered favorable signs for its evolution. Yet corruption, beginning at the top, remained rampant, the bureaucracy and elites mostly predatory in their relations with the peasants. Greed was to replace terror as the means of governing Haiti.

Internally some politics was permitted but not much. Dissident publications, a human rights movement, and embryonic trade unions and political parties were formed between 1976 and 1980 with some encouragement from the prohuman rights Carter administration in Washington. At the same time occasional expulsions, arbitrary arrests, and the uncovering of "plots" all occurred.

The 1979 legislative elections proved a litmus test of the regime's willingness to permit even a tame opposition. Using bribes, police, and threats the government swept all the seats except one from Cap Haïtien. Upset by the emergence of fledgling political parties, the government arrested nearly 200 persons on November 29, 1980, beginning a series of expulsions and show trials meant to destroy the semilegal opposition. It acted expecting that the newly elected Reagan administration would be less concerned for human rights in Haiti than its predecessor.

Economic recession, a massive illegal exodus of refugees, and political insecurity have characterized Haiti since 1980. Hit by the world recession, poor export prices, and tremendous internal problems, the economy falters. Lack of land, jobs, and opportunities prompted thousands of Haitians to take their chances in small boats headed toward Florida. Meanwhile the presidential family continues to line its pockets. The harassed local political opposition has temporarily taken a back seat to poorly organized exile invaders. None yet show significant internal support. Like its predecessors, the regime and family dynasty of Jean-Claude Duvalier found itself devoting much of its energies toward its own survival.

CONCLUSIONS

The second century of Haitian independence has been politically bleak. The U.S. occupation contributed to strengthening the control of the first world of Haiti over the second. No longer would regional revolts threaten the regime. Furthermore, the shock of white domination drove intellectuals of all colors and social backgrounds to question the course of Haitian politics and history as directed by elites in Port-au-Prince and to unite, at least temporarily, around an effort to validate the culture of the second world. This effort as well as the social changes occurring facilitated the rise of new black elites of a nonmilitary background.

The curbing of regional unrest by the U.S. marines during the occupation and a new respect for peasant black culture helped Dr. Duvalier take power and perpetuate his rule. Many of his methods were the same as his predecessors, but he was able to centralize control much better than they because of his ideology and his personal lack of moral restraint. Earlier administrations had to back down after the crowds of Port-au-Prince protested when they tried to change the constitution to stay in power. Duvalier unhesitatingly coopted or killed his opponents, drove them into exile, or silenced them in other ways before they could organize such demonstrations. A climate of fear and suspicion of one's neighbors, emphasis on personal security, a racial ideology, a government monopoly of weapons, and economic decline characterized a country best described by the novelist or poet. Haitian writer Anthony Phelps in his *Mémoire en Colin-Maillard* and British writer Graham Greene in his *The Comedians* captured the mindless terror and absurdity of the François Duvalier regime. The successor Duvalier regime has been less clear in its orientation. In some ways it has maintained its predecessor's methods and in other the older methods of political and economic control. The basic pattern of disrespect for institutions and an emphasis on personal ties persist over time. It is a system of "government by franchise."

NOTES

1. Dana G. Munro, *Intervention and Dollar Diplomacy in the Caribbean 1900–1921* (Westport, Conn: Greenwood, 1980; reprint of 1964 Princeton book), pp. 25–26.

2. Cited by Rayford W. Logan, *The Diplomatic Relations of the United States with Haiti 1776–1981* (Chapel Hill: University of North Carolina, 1941), p. 328.

3. Hans Schmidt, *The United States Occupation of Haiti 1915–1934* (New Brunswick: Rutgers University Press, 1971), pp. 4, 5–6. Unless otherwise noted, we are depending on Schmidt for this discussion of the occupation.

4. See Suzy Castor, *La ocupación norteamericana de Haití y sus consecuencias (1915–1934)* (Mexico: Siglo Veintiuno, 1971).

5. Schmidt, *The U.S. Occupation of Haiti*, p. 41

6. Munro, *Intervention and Dollar Diplomacy*, p. 23.

7. Jacques Stéphen Alexis, *Compère Général Soleil*, 3rd ed. (Paris: Gallimard, 1955), p. 101, ftn. 1.

8. Roger Gaillard, *Les blancs débarquent: 1915 premier écrasement du Cacoisme*, 2nd edition. (Port-au-Prince: Roger Gaillard, 1982), pp. 68–77 and Castor, *La ocupación*, pp. 122–23.

9. Munro, *Intervention and Dollar Diplomacy*, p. 373.

10. Robert I. Rotberg with Christopher K. Clague, *Haiti: The Politics of Squalor* (Boston: Houghton Mifflin, 1971), p. 122.

11. Interview with Jean Dominique, 3 May 1982; Castor, *La ocupación*, pp. 142–143; and see Roger Gaillard, *Charlemagne Péralte le Caco*, vol. 6, *Les blancs débarquent 1918–1919*, (Port-au-Prince: Roger Gaillard, 1982).

12. Robert Debs Heinl, Jr. and Nancy Gordon Heinl, *Written in Blood: The Story of the Haitian People 1492–1971* (Boston: Houghton Mifflin, 1978), p. 483.

13. Dana G. Munro, *The United States and the Caribbean Republics* (Princeton: Princeton University Press, 1974), p. 102.

14. Mats Lundahl, *Peasants and Poverty: A Study of Haiti* (New York: St. Martin's Press, 1979), p. 301.

15. Ibid., p. 372.

16. Schmidt, *The U.S. Occupation of Haiti*, p. 138.

17. Raymond Leslie Buell, "The American Occupation of Haiti," *Information Service*, New York, Foreign Policy Association, vol. 5, (27 November–12 December 1929): 390.

18. Ibid., p. 373, and Raymond Leslie Buell, "Sugar and the Tariff," *Information Service*, New York, Foreign Policy Association, vol. 5 (29 May 1929): 103–120.

19. See Ellen Conroy Kennedy, ed. and trans., *The Negritude Poets: An Anthology of Translations from the French* (New York: The Viking Press, 1975).

20. See Donald E. Herdeck with Maurice A. Lubin et al., eds., *Caribbean Writers: A Bio-Bibliographical Critical Encyclopedia* (Washington, D.C.: Three Continents Press, 1979).

21. Jean Price-Mars, "Préface," in *La montagne ensorcelée*, Jacques Roumain (1931; reprinted, Port-au-Prince: Ateliers Fardin, n.d.), pp. 9–13.

22. Jean Price-Mars, *La vocation de l'élite* (1919; reprinted, Port-au-Prince:

Ateliers Fardin, 1976). See Jacques C. Antoine, *Jean Price-Mars and Haiti* (Washington, D.C.: Three Continents, 1981), p. 116.

23. Jean Price-Mars, *Lettre ouverte au Dr. René Piquion* (Port-au-Prince: Editions des Antilles, 1967), p. 33.

24. See David Nicholls, *From Dessalines to Duvalier: Race, Colour and National Independence in Haiti* (Cambridge: Cambridge University Press, 1979) pp. 165–81; and J. Michael Dash, *Literature and Ideology in Haiti 1915–1916* (Totowa, New Jersey: Barnes and Noble, 1981), pp. 51–90, 99–113.

25. Ulrich Fleischmann, "Le Créole en voie de devenir une langue littér-aire," in *Littératures et langues dialectales françaises,* ed. Dieter Kremer and Hans-Josef Niederehe, (Hamburg: Helmut Buske, 1979), p. 258; and Dash, *Lit. and Ideology in Haiti,* p. 140.

26. Heinl, *Written in Blood,* pp. 528–30.

27. Colonel D.P. Calixte, *Haiti: The Calvary of a Soldier* (New York: Wendell Malliet, 1939).

28. See Rayford W. Logan, *Haiti and the Dominican Republic* (New York: Oxford, 1968), pp. 145–46.

29. Heinl, *Written in Blood,* p. 537.

30. Ibid., pp. 539–40.

31. Mirlande Hippolyte-Manigat, *Haiti and the Caribbean Community: Profile of an Applicant and the Problematique of Widening the Integration Movement,* trans. K.Q. Warner (Kingston, Jamaica; Institute of Social and Economic Research, University of the West Indies, 1980), p. 156. And, Monique P. Garrity, "The Multinational Corporation in Extractive Industries: A Case Study of Reynolds Haitians Mines, Inc.," in *Working Papers in Haitian Society and Culture,* ed. Sidney M. Mintz (New Haven: Yale University Antilles Research Program, 1975), pp. 183–290.

32. Castor, *La ocupación,* pp. 214–215, wrote that Estimé's talk of promoting the black masses was no more than demagogy which helped a growing black middle class legitimize its power.

33. Nicholls, *From Dessalines to Duvalier,* p. 191.

34. Haiti government debt rose from $3–4 million at the start of the Magloire presidency to $40 million in 1957. See Leslie F. Manigat, *Haiti of the Sixties, Object of International Concern* (Washington: The Washington Center of Foreign Policy Research, 1964), pp. 75–76.

35. Heinl, *Written in Blood,* p. 582.

36. Lorimer Denis and Dr. François Duvalier, *Problème des classes à travers l'historie d'Haiti* (Port-au-Prince: Collection 'Les Griots', 1948), p. 3.

37. Ibid., p. 17.

38. Ibid., p. 103.

39. Ibid., p. 105.

40. Ibid., pp. 110–11.

41. Heinl, *Written in Blood,* p. 600.

42. Christian A. Girault, *Le commerce du café en Haïti: Habitants, spéculateurs et exportateurs* (Paris: CNRS, 1981), p. 155

43. Lundahl, *Peasants and Poverty,* pp. 377–82.

44. Nicholls, *From Dessalines to Duvalier,* p. 212.

45. Gérard Campfort, "Enjeu éducatif en Haïti," (Mémoire, Université de paris I, 1976), p. 59. Interview with Jean Dominique, 31 May 1983.

46. See Bertrand de la Grange, "Haïti à la dérive," *Le Monde,* 30 May 1981, p. 1.

47. It sparked the publication of a response by Charles Manigat, Claude Moise and Emile Ollivier, *Haïti: Quel développement-Propos sur l'enquête de Jean-Jacques Honorat* (Montreal: Collectif Paroles, 1975).

48. Jean-Jacques Honorat, *Enquête sur le développement,* (Port-au-Prince: Imprimerie Centrale, 1974), pp. 217–18.

3

INSTITUTIONS:
GOVERNMENT BY FRANCHISE

Twenty-five years of Duvalier family rule have not given the republic an all-powerful central government capable of penetrating most corners of national life. Nor can we say that specific directives from Port-au-Prince are responsible for all existing patterns of exploitation and oppression. Most rulers have sought only to maintain themselves in power and to extract sufficient funds from the population and foreign donors for their personal bank accounts and safety. They have been indifferent to the usual obligations of modern government: public transportation is nonexistent; public schools are considered a disaster; farmers expect no advice, low interest loans, technical assistance, protection against exporters, or irrigation schemes. Victims of natural disasters, oppressive treatment by Dominican planters or local employers, passengers on marooned ships, and interns in foreign prisons can expect assistance only from their own families, friends and foreigners acting through private voluntary organizations and sometimes through foreign governments. Agendas for development, which always include expansion of government services, are drawn up by foreign aid officials, some local intellectuals, and a few highly competent but frustrated Haitian civil servants who come and go. The ruling family acquiesces in them as long as they can still pursue their own well-defined financial and security interests unhindered. Any project or person who seems to benefit

the country as a whole but adversely affects Duvalier interests will be blocked.

Nonetheless, Haitians feel the weight of the state; and they are fully aware of the barriers erected to prevent them from participating in power, wealth, and prestige. The key to understanding this system is what we call "government by franchise." Government by franchise involves the assignment of government functions to trusted persons and families within the central government, in cities and throughout the rural areas. At present, acting under the sanction of the center or of President Jean-Claude Duvalier himself, these Haitians ensure the flow of resources from the rural to the urban worlds, and they maintain security in areas they generally know quite well. In return they are allowed to purchase coffee, lend money, seize land, and hire their relatives and friends with whom they rule a ministry, a town, or a rural section, extracting benefits for themselves as they can and as they will. Beyond the minimum requirements of resources and security as defined by the central rulers, local authorities are quite free from outside control to pursue their own financial and security interests. Flying the Duvalier black and red flag and carrying the small arms allowed to them, they rule the country. Churches, foreign supported charitable organizations, and other private foreign donors carry a major responsibility for health, education, and other services. Experts in public administration might call this a centralized but deconcentrated regime: the source of all power and legitimacy is the presidental palace, but, within limits, the day to day decisions are made by thousands of individuals throughout the country.

Holders of these local "franchises" are not linked together horizontally in any one organization. Each has his or her own narrow network which carefully excludes nonmembers from participation and is linked vertically with the president. They often compete or enter into conflict with each other, but together they provide a political infrastructure for the whole country, in which most of the population has no share.

A minimum hourly wage of $0.33, extremely high rates of unemployment, an ill-adapted educational system, heavy export taxes borne by coffee growers, high import taxes on basic commodities, and a generally regressive tax system help maintain the barriers to participation in wealth. Access to information, an important aspect of participation, is very limited. If a worker wishes to purchase the Labor Code, which allegedly protects workers, he or she must be prepared to spend $12.00, a week's wages. The two-volume budget of Haiti costs $25.00 and the official journal of laws and decrees will cost about $0.40 per page at the National Printers. These sums of money are beyond the reach of the workers, who, in any case, read cannot French, the language of these documents. Nor are they available in libraries or other public places. Refusal to use Creole in schools and in government documents even though this is the true national language understood by all citizens helps maintain ignorance, limits job opportunities, and is a symbol of disdain for peasant culture, the demagogy about "our African ancestors" and the "noble peasants" notwithstanding.

One slim promise of participation in wealth is the state lottery. "Borlette" is a daily phenomenon, much like the numbers game in U.S. cities played by the poor in hopes of making their fortune. Prizes can be quite large. On May 28, 1982, the grand prize of the "Venezuela" lottery reached Gds 135,000 or about $27,000, but the winner in this case was the lottery itself, a frequent occurrence. Poor Haitians take their chances on the lottery even though the deck is stacked against them.

The only hope to participate in the economic and political system is to establish personal ties with the powerful and the rich. Power is personalized at all levels, and links between the center and the provinces are not institutional. If one has the family and friendship ties with those in power, one's interests will be safeguarded and one will be respected; if not, one is excluded from participation and plays the role of victim of government and business. Thus, prosperous families try to place a relative in a key ministry and in the officer corps of the army. At every level in this society personalization is the key to power and resources.

CONSTITUTIONS

Constitutions in Haiti are personal charters of current rulers. New heads of state regularly have refashioned the document to suit their immediate needs and interests. Consequently, Haiti has had over twenty constitutions since the first in 1801. This preindependence charter made Toussaint Louverture governor general. Several constitutions, beginning with the next one, the independence or Dessalines constitution of 1805, reenforced the personalization of Haitian politics by praising the president by name, giving him life tenure, as in the Duvalier constitution of 1964, or calling him the personification of the Haitian nation.

All constitutions reflect the desire of the head of state to accumulate power, permitting him to relegate the legislature, the courts, and other institutions to a secondary position if he chooses. The related issue of presidential tenure arises each time the constitution is revised, and succession is a constant theme: should the term of office be for four or more years; should the president be allowed to succeed himself, name his successor, or rule for life. Solutions vary, but no head of state has felt constrained by constitutions, even his own.

The question of land ownership has appeared in constitutions since 1805 in a negative or positive form. Dessalines introduced a provision forbidding foreign ownership, but President Salomon favored a law in 1883 which permitted foreign agricultural enterprises to invest.[1] Antiforeign provisions prevailed until 1918 when the U.S. occupation authorities removed them from their own Haitian constitution. Writers of subsequent constitutions, including the one now in force, have addressed the question of foreign ownership. Since the advent of the Duvaliers the constitution actually encouraged non-Haitians to purchase land although changes in 1983 made this somewhat ambiguous.

Universal suffrage and direct election of the president and legislature came to Haiti in the twentieth century. Alexandre Pétion, who ruled the southern half of the country when it was split in two parts, limited suffrage in his 1816 constitution to men who were neither servants nor peasants, which, Leyburn says, meant that about 3 percent of the population was eligible to participate in the electoral process.[2] Traditionally, the lower house of the legislature was elected by town notables. The lower house then selected the upper house from a list presented to it by the head of state. The legislature had the task of selecting presidents. It was not until 1950 that Haitians voted directly for their president. In short, until quite recently only a tiny minority in Port-au-Prince participated in the electoral process.

The Toussaint constitution of 1801, Dessalines in 1805, and Christophe in 1807 and 1811, introduced and maintained forced labor. The provision disappeared, but a law permitting forced labor to build roads was passed in 1864. U.S. occupation authorities revived it after 1915.[3]

Almost all constitutions have affirmed republican principles since the reunification of Haiti in 1820 and the demise of the northern kingdom belonging to Christophe. Soulouque's constitution of 1849 which created the Second Empire was the exception.

Not unexpectedly, President François Duvalier rewrote the constitution after his election in 1957. He did so again in 1961, and then in 1964 to make himself president for life; and he amended it in 1971 shortly before his death to ensure that his young son would succeed him. In 1983 it was rewritten again. This high-minded document recognizes the need for social justice, a Haitian-style democracy, and efficient administration.[4]

Seven articles deal with foreigners living in Haiti, including their economic rights. Foreigners are excluded from retail trade. This provision came from decrees issued in 1807 and 1809, but this has not prevented the intrusion of Syrians and Lebanese.

Another economic and social concern expressed is that each worker should have an annual paid vacation. The state is supposed to encourage marriage, particularly among peasants. This latter provision reflects a concern to penetrate Haitian peasant society by sanctioning marriage and reducing the system of plaçage or common law marriages, one technique peasants use to avoid dealing with the government.

Since changes in 1961 the constitution limits the legislature to one house instead of the usual two, calling it the "Legislative Chamber" (Constitution: Chapter II). Today a minimum of 59 members take their places for a six-year term after election by universal suffrage of all Haitians 18 and older. The assembly may be adjourned by the president, and it may be dissolved by the president before expiration of the term. Members meet for three or four months beginning in April and receive a salary determined by the annual budget (Art. 87).

Articles dealing with the president are most interesting. His powers are extensive and open to enlargement. The legislature can grant the president "full powers" allowing him to suspend constitutional guarantees of human rights, for example.[5] In the François Duvalier constitution the president names all civil servants to their posts; he is the guarantor of both internal and external security (Art. 92). Article 99, introduced in 1964, confirmed "Citizen Doctor François Duvalier" president for life because, among other accomplishments, he "laid the basis for national prosperity" and "undertook and succeeded in eradicating illiteracy." This panegyric has, of course, absolutely no truth. Article 100 specifically allows Dr. Duvalier to name his successor who will also be president for life (Art. 104) and the 1983 constitution allows his son to name the next president for life (Art. 107, 108). The salary of the head of state is a minuscule Gds 10,000 or $2,000 per month (Art. 97).

The president names all judges, but the latter are supposed to have a ten-year term which cannot be interrupted except for reasons to be established by law. The constitution creates a supreme court or Cour de Cassation, courts of appeal, lower courts, as well as military courts. The different jurisdiction between civilian and military courts is not clear.

Section VIII guarantees free enterprise (Art. 163) and promises that the state will help families to own their own houses.[6] In a section on the family, revealing articles reflect Haitian concerns and Haitian realities: husband and wife are politically and economically equal; recognizing that probably the majority of children in Haiti are born to parents whose marriage has not been sanctioned by church or state, the constitution declares that parents must provide for all their children—"legitimate and natural children legally recognized..." (Art. 171). Article 172 states that a law will determine how paternity is established, and even if paternity is not established, the state itself has obligations to all children. It must "protect the physical, mental and moral health of minors and guarantee their right to help and to education." (Art. 174). Unlike most other countries, the Haitian constitution explicitly forbids schools to discriminate against children on the basis of whether their parents are married or on the basis of their color, religion, or social status (Art. 182). The old and the poor can count on the solicitude of the state, according to Article 179. The constitution calls for respect for Haitian culture, the "Trésor Haïtien" (Art. 184).[7]

In sum, Haiti's constitution is in many ways a very progressive document reflecting and promoting many principles relevant to the people's lives. On the other hand, it sets up a highly personalized, authoritarian system which can disregard those principles. The lowering of the minimum age for the president from 40 to 18 in the January 14, 1971 revision to permit Jean-Claude Duvalier to succeed his father shows how personal the document is. Very few Haitians have read the constitution. The day to day Haitian realities bear no resemblance to the progressive aspects of the charter or the current slogans of what is called *jean-claudisme*. The Duvalier family rules the country without attention to constitution or ideology but with sharp attention to their "franchise" relationships with administrators at all levels from department to rural sections.

FROM DEPARTEMENT TO SECTION RURALE

The president has available three types of franchise he can offer to supporters: military, civilian, and militia. None has a well-articulated hierarchy or clear personnel policy. The essential rule is that many officials report directly to the president or indirectly through the Department of the Interior and National Defense, which, as the name indicates, has charge of both civilian and military administration.

The largest administrative units into which Haiti is divided are thus military districts or *départements*. Prior to 1957 there were five, now there are nine. A solider at the rank of colonel is usually in charge of this unit, but changes in the constitution during 1983 provided for a civilian prefect.

It is too early to determine what the results will be. The department is further divided into military *districtes* headed by a captain. Districts are divided into subdistricts headed by a lieutenant. The duties of the military are more important than the duties of the civilians, including the control of traffic and trade, enforcing laws relating to security, control of prisons, and intelligence activities. They are also supposed to organize relief operations during catastrophes. A chief of staff is the nominal head of the military, but even low-level command units can accept direct orders only from the president.[8]

The largest civilian administrative unit corresponds more or less with the military district, but is smaller; it is called the *arrondissement.* There are 27 arrondissements each of which is headed by a civilian prefect who is mainly supposed to supervise the activities of the technical ministries such as education and agriculture. Civil and criminal courts are located in the main town of the arrondissement.

The next largest unit is the commune. At times in Haiti's history the communes elected their council and mayor, but the first postoccupation constitution of 1935 gave the president the right to appoint the mayor of every commune. During the 1940s the commune regained some autonomy, both political and financial, but Duvalier reinstituted patterns of dependence and the importance of personal ties between head of state and local officials. Each town has a council in addition to the mayor. Throughout the Duvalier period councillors and mayors were appointed by the president or with his approval. The first municipal elections in more than 30 years were held in 1983 with most of the elected mayors supporting the president. An independent candidate was elected in Cap Haïtien.[9]

These first carefully controlled municipal elections are unlikely to lead to a strengthening of local government, at least in the shortrun. A law passed in 1958 transferred funds controlled by towns to the Department of the Interior: "the same law authorized the Secretary of the Interior to use all the money for the secret police, contrary to the law of 1944 which divided this surplus in useful projects for the community."[10] Thus, the newly elected mayors and councillors are still dependent on the central government for economic resources.

Located in each commune are a justice of the peace, the main school, army barracks, and a tax collection office. Attached to each of the 131 communes are *Sections Rurales* (rural sections), the heart of the country's administration, both civilian and military.

The 555 Sections Rurales are the most important manifestation of the central government for over 4 million rural Haitians. The person in charge of the section is officially called the Chef de Section. Peasants call him "commandant" or even "L'eta" (The State). He is the lowest ranking official of the civilian and the military structure, and without his loyalty the system could not operate. Historically, the military chiefs of staff named the "commandant," but Dr. Duvalier chose these key figures himself, and the tradition continues with his son. Although a rural code is supposed to govern the chef's activities, duties, and responsibilities, the only important requirement is loyalty to the head of state, the maintenance of order, and the extraction of resources.

The chef controls an area of about forty square kilometers with up to 20,000 inhabitants. He is supposed to keep current records of births and deaths. Peasants may call upon him to settle disputes, and to draw up an witness contracts if they have some confidence in him. He is probably a native of the section, already an important landholder, middleman or coffee *spéculateur,* and a relative of the previous chef. Many chefs lend money and use their position to purchase agricultural products for resale. It is a very attractive job. At least two assistants run the chef's office from day to day. More assistants, responsible for the smaller zones, called "habitations" or "bouquements" into which the section is unofficially divided, report to him. Each assistant controls about ten police agents. In the section where Pnina Lahav conducted her research there was one police agent for every 240 persons, not counting the militia.[11] This means that each chef de section can choose about 100 persons to work under his command. They are relatives and friends for the most part.

It is crucial for an understanding of Haitian institutions to know that in the 1970s the chef received a derisory salary of 150 gourdes or $30 per month and that his 100 subordinates were not paid at all. Furthermore, they are all subject to military law and courts, not civilian courts. As a result, the officials at the level of section must extract their incomes from the local population by whatever means they can, and the local populace has no protection in the courts. This is not an innovation, for Dessalines similarly "left his army to feed and clothe itself."[12] Because all are subject to military courts, known for their harshness and arbitrary judgments, there is a certain amount of fear in relationships within the administration. The head of a subsection can imprison the chef de section without much pretext. Thus, decisions and behavior between administrators can be just as capricious as between administration and populace. Because the system operates on the basis of personal loyalty to the head of state, Jean-Claude Duvalier replaced many chefs de section after taking power in 1971.

SECURITY FORCES

The third pillar of the administration for the Duvalier family is the VSN militia, the Volontaires de la Sécurité Nationale, or tontons macoutes. They patrol the countryside, maintain checkpoints on the roads, and circulate quietly in the towns in their blue uniforms and dark glasses. Of the three groups they are the most likely to be illiterate except for the officers. Estimates of their number range all the way from 5,000 to 10,000.

One observer called the VSN a "parabureaucracy" because one of their tasks is to keep the rest of the bureaucracy loyal to the Duvaliers. Their sole raison d'etre is to protect the interests of the ruling family, and for this reason they are better equipped than the army. Once a year they make the following pledge:

> I swear to defend, alongside the armed forces of Haiti, the integrity of the national territory, to police and ensure the security of towns and countryside, to watch the coasts and frontiers and to obey the head of state, who is the supreme guardian of the moral and material interests of the nation.[13]

They serve to neutralize the army, which Dr. Duvalier always perceived as a potential threat. Spying on civilians, the military, and other administrators seems to be their main function, and they report to the office of the president. They also spy on each other. Delince, a former Haitian army officer now in exile, reports that each VSN unit has one member who makes secret reports on the loyalty of his colleagues and probably other units. The VSN is more divided than the army, and each unit jealously guards the area under its command. A reason for the lack of coordination may be that when the VSN was first created in 1962, its leader eventually turned against Dr. Duvalier, posing a serious threat to him. The president approved all members of the VSN and selected some. Because Jean-Claude Duvalier cannot know each individual, he depends on the judgment and recommendations of key VSN personnel, who naturally recommend relatives and friends. This responsibility gives them a larger stake in the system.

The decree establishing the VSN specifies that members are not to be paid although some observers report that company commanders are. In any case, the VSN, like other administrators, extracts most of its remuneration from the populace. One source of income is a type of protection racket. Individual tontons macoutes or units earn their living by "protecting" merchants against some imagined threat. The threat often comes from the VSN itself but may also come from the section police or military who are on the lookout for money. A common sight on lucrative Saturday nights is the VSN, revolver in full view, who has arrived for his payment from bartenders, dance hall keepers, and restauranteurs.

As in the case of some chefs de section, it appears that the young Duvalier wished to replace or even neutralize the VSN with his own loyalists. This may be one reason he created an elite presidential military unit of 500 or 600 men called the "Leopards." Internal security is also their primary task.

The weak may try to play off the strong against each other as one form of defense. In one rural section a member of the VSN killed a peasant after a fight at a dance. The dead man's family, tenant farmers, begged the landowner, a man with some prestige in the area, to help them. The landowner, who told the authors he felt some paternal responsibility, turned to the military head of the subdistrict who summoned the tonton macoute for a superficial harangue to impress the landowner. Nonetheless, the guilty party promised to pay the widow about $60, enough for burial expenses. There was obviously no question of going to court. Everything was done in a personal, noninstitutional way.

More serious for the future of the regime is that these military and quasi-military units fight among themselves, often killing each other in significant numbers. In recent years reports of shoot-outs between Leopards and VSN in Port-au-Prince and between the military and the VSN in a provincial town have been confirmed. The confrontations develop out of petty disputes and apparently worry the occupants of the presidential palace. On the other hand, such conflicts could deter any serious military opposition from growing as long as they are kept at a relatively low level. The president can even play the role of mediator.

From the point of view of the poorest peasant and worker there is little difference between the VSN, the military, the Chef de Section, and the businessman or woman. Exploitation and intimidation of the people at the bottom are the norm. Exploitation provides these agents with an income, and intimidation gives them a sense of their own importance—which they need because they are being intimidated by someone else, higher up—while keeping the countryside and towns quiet. As long as they can act in the name of the state or the Duvalier family, and as long as they monopolize small arms, the Chefs de Section and the VSN keep the system afloat. Any threat to the Duvalier regime is a threat to them, their families and friends, and altogether they are an important percentage of the population.

Many people claim to act in the name of the state, even if they are not paid by the state. About 30,000 civilian and military personnel are supposed to be paid directly by the state, "supposed" because at times they have gone for a few months without being paid due to budgetary deficits. One-fourth of state employees are military or approximately 6,500. In addition, there are possibly 50,000 rural police unpaid by the state plus the thousands of VSN. In short, there must be 90,000 men and women who speak and act in the name of Duvalier's Haiti. Adding to them their families and close friends, as well as those who have been or hope to be employed by the state, the total could be 10 percent of the population, a substantial group, particularly since it is much better organized than anyone else.

Because the Haitian state traditionally has intervened in the economy only to extract money, production and marketing have been left completely in the hands of peasants and an important group of entrepreneurs. The latter purchase coffee for resale to the exporters, and they purchase food for resale in Port-au-Prince. Girault estimates that there are 750 men licensed to purchase coffee from the peasants and then to resell it to the export houses.[14] In addition there are over a thousand illegal middlemen who buy and sell. Some of them are members of the VSN, chefs de section, or local merchants. Food crops such as rice are purchased by women, called "Madan Saras" (Creole) or "Madame Sarahs" (French). Haitian geographer, Georges Anglade, has studied the marketing of coffee destined for export and the marketing of food destined for local consumption, and he believes that there are "1,300 Madan Saras who transport more than 1,000 tons of agricultural produce to Port-au-Prince every day." They sell this food to about 50,000 retailers.[15]

Both the men in coffee marketing and the women in food are political actors. During the rebellion by Charlemagne Péralte against the American occupation the Madan Saras, who travel through the countryside to and from urban areas, spread the message of Péralte and transmitted information to him about U.S. troop movements.[16] Under François Duvalier some of the Madan Saras joined the coffee middlemen in the tonton macoute or were protected by the tonton macoute. Like those who hold the political franchise the coffee middlemen and food middlewomen along with merchants, landlords, and moneylenders hold a type of economic franchise and thus identify their fate with the continuing existence of the regime in Port-au-Prince. They have received tangible social and economic benefits from the Duvaliers. They have seen black symbols validated; some of their children moved into the first world through education and appointment; and they gained control over an important source of income.

An attempt to overthrow the president is seen as an attempt to remove all those who hold some kind of franchise from the president. Thus, they are ready to put down the least hint of opposition with extreme brutality. Their own insecurity and unsureness about what constitutes a threat to the regime pushes them to err on the side of force. Haitians commonly say that if one complains he or she is hungry, reports will be made to the VSN or police who may interpret this as a political statement and proceed to abuse them physically. If the tontons macoutes put them into prison, there is no guarantee of a meal either.

The Duvalier family keeps the various forces divided and suspicious of each other. Delince uses the words anarchy, insecurity, cliques, factions, and fear to describe the mentality of these forces who must worry that they could be denounced by colleagues for disloyalty.[17] The ruling family takes other measures for their physical security. In the capital itself they maintain a presidential guard of five companies (a company in Haiti contains from 120 to 200 persons). These men live in the presidential palace, where heavy weapons are stored. In case of a military attack on the palace the guard would be able to defend it with weapons not available elsewhere in the country. There is a separate police force for Port-au-Prince and a Service Détectif operating out of the Dessalines Barracks near the presidential palace. Composed of about "300 civilian detectives and undercover agents" their job is to discover alleged traitors and plotters.[18] Lastly, it is very likely the government sends agents overseas to report on Haitian émigré activities in the United States, Canada, and France. Such agents also work within foreign organizations and embassies making reports on their activities, plans, and gossip to the president or the ministry of the interior.

CENTRAL ADMINISTRATION

Ministries in the capital operate in much the same way as rural administrations. They provide jobs for friends and relatives of the ministers, and together they form a coterie around the Duvalier family. Personnel in the ministries resist change and consider secrecy one of their best protections. Serge Vieux put it best when he wrote that the Haitian administration is "non-functional" with respect to the tasks it is allegedly to perform,[19] but it helps maintain the present distribution of power and wealth.

Each ministry or department, as it is called, is a world unto itself, and each change of minister involves the movement in and out of a significant number of the workers. Before the new civil service law was passed, each newly installed department head determined hiring and firing rules. There had been no standard examination system or clear-cut published list of educational requirements. Although there is a school of public administration which is supposed to prepare Haitians or to retrain them for jobs in the civil service, analysts complain about the low level of competence of government employees. Perhaps the reason is that approximately "75 percent of all new appointments are based on some form of patronage or sponsorship."[20] Thus, like the Chef de Section, the head of a department surrounds himself with friends and relatives whose interests are then bound together with the interests of the Duvalier family. They work to maintain the peace and support for the government in the capital and within their particular administration in the provinces.

President Jean-Claude Duvalier has encouraged departmental patronage more than his father. Frequent ministerial changes give hope to many they will soon be on or back on the payroll. (An observer calculated that the average life of a ministerial appointment is slightly more than 200 days.) Increased foreign assistance for development projects and ordinary government services frees domestically generated income for salaries. In the decade of Jean-Claude Duvalier's rule the number of civil servants officially and openly paid from public funds increased "from 15,604 for the fiscal year 1970–71 to 29,318 for the fiscal year 1980–81."[21] Their average salary also increased from $50 per month to $125 per month.

THE BUDGET

The budget explicitly provides substantial discretionary funds for ministries, thus permitting considerable flexibility in hiring practices. The total discretionary spending under Jean-Claude Duvalier has risen from $400,000 a year to $4,000,000 a year.[22] It is not clear whether these funds pay the salaries of the bureaucrats added since 1970–71 or whether they are used for yet additional personnel. In any case, we can safely assume that the minister takes a substantial slice from it for his personal bank account. The money appears in part in the budget under the rubric "without justification." In 1981–82, for example, the Department of Foreign Affairs received $450,000 "sans justification," the presidency $550,000, the prefects, who can fend for themselves, a modest $50,000, and general administration $600,000.[23]

One important category in the annual expenditures of the government of Haiti is the Caisse Centrale d'Amortissement (Debt Repayment Fund) which receives about $53 million out of total annual expenditures of $171 million, almost one-third. The Caisse Centrale is responsible for paying Haiti's debts and obligations. Slightly more than $7 million is allocated for interest and public debt and another $1.4 million for the debt of the state-run electric company. Many expenditures are explained in a very vague way, and almost $9 million a year is allocated to the famous Régie du Tabac et des Allumettes.[24]

The Tobacco Office is an independent public body which is the bane of all foreign aid agencies. The main sources of Régie income are commissions on the sale of flour, sugar, and cement as well as on tobacco, cigarettes, and matches, but everyone complains it does not account for the substantial sum received from the budget and its own methods of collection. Total revenues have been estimated at about $15 million a year of which probably two-thirds go directly to the ruling family. International lending agencies, USAID, and other bilateral donors have been unable to pressure the Haitian authorities to transfer Régie money to the development budget. Of the whole tax and budget process foreign officials have complained "it is impossible to present a complete picture of Haitian public finance."[25]

The financial procedures of any particular department are equally inscrutable. One outside study of the Department of Health discovered that:

> thirty-one separate steps involving a host of actors both within and outside the ministry are required in order to disburse funds. Even the initial determination of the availability of money is clouded. It appears that the chief of accounting makes such a determination according to criteria that are largely undocumented and unknown to others.[26]

Keeping disbursement methods a secret or making them extremely complicated is a method to prevent outside control and is a guarantee of freedom for those in charge. Without such a guarantee, the loyalty of the minister and his close circle of associates would be doubtful. The appointment in early 1982 of Marc Bazin, a respected Haitian official at the World Bank, as Secretary for Financial Affairs seemed to promise a measure of order, honesty, and rationality. He succeeded in initiating some reforms and dismissed officials known to be corrupt. He is given credit for exposing the stolen automobile trade. As soon as he touched the critical interests of the rulers and business families by trying to force payment of income taxes, he was blocked and fired. His growing popularity was also perceived as a personal threat to the president, who is always on guard against *Dauphins.*

The ministers have several techniques to ensure the personal loyalty of subordinates. A civil servant who takes a leave of absence for any legitimate reason, including further study, can never be sure his job will be kept for him. A second means of control is through the pension policy or lack of pension policy. Although money is deducted from salaries for retirement programs, no civil servant can be sure he will receive a pension. Each pension must be negotiated with the minister and other high ranking officials. Obviously, if one has displeased the minister, one has no hope of a decent retirement. It is anyone's guess where the deducted money goes, but the practice of explained or unexplained deductions also prevails in private industry, where workers say they do not understand the accounting system. Asking many questions means loss of the job; going on strike could mean loss of life.

Insecurity of tenure and pensions plus the low pay forces civil servants to look for additional sources of revenue. Common practice is finding another job within the bureaucracy. (Authors of a study found one person with five different positions in the civil service.) In rural areas civil servants may lend money and buy and sell commodities. A result is that the functionary is often absent from the assigned job. In addition, the low salaries open up the administration to penetration by those who bribe civil servants in order to obtain administrative decisions in their favor. Although less free than Chefs de Section who are far from the capital, administrators dealing with the public in Port-au-Prince are tempted to demand payment for tasks they are supposed to do as civil servants, including the simple supply of information.

Under the pressure from the Americans and international lending agencies to introduce reforms, Duvalier created an Administrative Reform Commission in 1974. It was reorganized in 1981. The Commission proposed several basic changes, including "fiscal and budgetary reform," civil service modernization and regional planning.[27] In August 1982 the government proposed a civil service law, and it was passed. If it is enforced, it could improve the situation and security of civil servants. The government also dismissed 35 employees of the very important customs service and announced the appointment of replacements with a reputation for technical competence and probity.[28] The president also upgraded the Conseil National de Développement et du Plan into a ministry of planning in 1978 as part of what the head of state calls his economic revolution, and the country is currently following its third general development plan to last from 1981 to 1986. The current plan is directed at rural development; it could not function, as earlier indicated, without foreign financial assistance.

Urban ruling elites and government are largely indifferent to rural development and rural education. Traditionally, the "provinces" have been among the most materially deprived in the Western Hemisphere. For a total rural population of about 4.5 million there are currently 131 farm agents and 55 home economists according to outside observers. But, it is in education and the status of the Creole language where government shows itself most indifferent to the needs of Haiti's second world.

EDUCATIONAL INSTITUTIONS

Results of surveys and interviews show that Haitians of all classes want their children to complete their formal education in French in order to take their place in society as professionals or civil servants. They realize their children do poorly in schools and soon drop out but are unsure why.[29] The number and quality of teachers is one reason. In 1980–81 there were 14,900 primary school teachers in Haiti of which 5,500 taught in public schools and 9,400 in private schools. The average rural public school teacher has from 75–100 students in a class.[30] Although public school teachers' salaries were recently raised from $60 per month to $100 per month, they still receive $25 less than the average civil servant. A teaching career is unattractive to talented and ambitious individuals who look for other positions. (Private school teachers earn only $40 per month.) Most rural teachers have completed only a few grades more than their students and are not competent in French, the only officially permitted medium of instruction until 1979.

More than half of Haiti's children are enrolled in private schools. Probably the best and the worst schools in Haiti are private. The best have been church-run, most often Roman Catholic. Many other private schools are the property of an older teacher or a group of teachers. Middle class and worker parents make great sacrifices to pay school fees, particularly in private schools. Public schools have had a bad reputation throughout Haitian history, but the situation is so difficult for some private institutions that "22 percent...operate in the open air, without buildings."[31]

Either because of inadequate school facilities, (overcrowding, no nearby school at all, unhealthy conditions), the inability of parents to pay public school fees of $18.00, irrelevant and uninteresting curricula, incompetent teachers, or language problems, school enrollments are extremely low. In 1978 only 24 percent of all children aged 6 to 11 were in school.

Breaking the data into rural and urban, figures are 62 percent urban and only 14 percent rural.[32]

More alarming are the data indicating a drastic current dropout rate. Although 48 percent of the eligible rural children (about 6 years old) attend the first year of primary school, by the second year 18 percent are present, and by the fourth year 8.5 percent. Only about 3 percent of the rural students who begin school will complete the primary cycle.[33] This is stark proof of indifference toward rural development.

At the secondary school level about 52,250 students attend classes in 146 establishments.[34] Only 5,694 young men and women are enrolled in vocational schools (figures are probably incomplete) and 3,081 in the State University of Haiti, the only university in the country.[35] Since five years of schooling are necessary to produce a literate child, the high dropout rate and low levels of attendance ensure a continuing 80 percent higher rate of illiteracy in Haiti.

In recent years analysts have blamed a curriculum unrelated to the experience and needs of the people, and teaching methods which emphasize memorization and French for the dismal state of education. Visitors to the republic have often been amazed and perplexed observing children and adolescents sitting under a streetlight mumbling their lessons which they are trying to learn by heart in preparation for examinations to come.

THE QUESTION OF CREOLE

The issue of Creole is directly related to problems in education and participation in the political and economic systems of Haiti. For the last forty years the place of this language has been openly debated. Earlier in this century Price-Mars warned his compatriots that the exclusive use of French from the first day of school to the last day barred the way to an effective education, particularly for the monolingual Creole-speaking lower classes. He believed that if educationists would admit that Creole, not French, was the pupil's mother tongue, they would first use Creole as a medium of instruction, then teach French as a foreign language before using it to teach arithmetic or history.[36] This technique would probably enlarge rural access to education, but Price-Mars knew urban elites feared such an outcome.

Georges Sylvain took a more forceful stand at about the same time. He proposed using Creole as the language of instruction and seemed less concerned to introduce French. Jules Faine, a participant in the Indigéniste movement studying and validating rural culture, expanded the argument.

In his book *Philologie créole,* published in 1939, he challenged all the prejudices surrounding the Haitian language by asserting that it is a tongue with its own grammar and not a corrupted dialect of French as some claimed. He politicized the matter further by calling Creole a symbol of Haitian identity and an appropriate instrument for administrative tasks.[37] Ever since, more and more people have discussed Creole, and ordinary Haitians now express pride and loyalty to their mother tongue. From 1979 to mid-1982 Sylvain's views showed signs of beginning to prevail, as we shall see. Non-Haitians such as Albert Valdman, an important American linguist, encouraged expanded use of Creole, as did some French and Canadian linguists; Valdman went further than most by calling for the coofficialization of Creole alongside French. One result of such action would be that peasants would have the right to communicate with government authorities and expect a response in written Creole. Another is that laws would be published in Creole. Competence in French—now limited to urban residents and rich landowners and rural middlemen—would no longer be the major qualification for civil service employment.

Studies by Haitian and foreign scholars have strengthened the case for Creole. The question of education through the mother tongue has been raised worldwide in Africa, India, and Latin America. UNESCO, many educators, linguists, and the World Bank[38] have supported the use of mother tongues as media of instruction. Fears of elites whose knowledge of the dominant language is one guarantee of their status, the often underdeveloped lexicon of mother tongues, and fears of monolingual masses themselves that the life chances of their children will be limited unless they can use French or English make the question more complicated in these countries.

In Haiti linguists have shown that the mother tongue of almost 100 percent of black and brown Haitians belongs to the Creole group of languages. Creoles, which are independent languages, develop over the centuries out of trade languages such as pidgins. Leyburn, Valdman, and others have explained the origins of Haitian Creole whose grammar is neither French nor African although the lexicon draws from French. Despite the lexical similarities, Creole is no more a dialect of French than is English which, thanks to the Normans, Chaucer, and others, also borrowed heavily from French. French-based though it largely is in vocabulary, Haitian Creole is an independent language with its own traditions, literature, styles, utility, and symbolic value. It is the exclusive means of communication for at least 85 percent of the population who cannot communicate in French. French has always been the only official language, however, since the day when Creole-speaking Jean-Jacques Dessalines approved the declaration of independence in French. More recently, the Duvalier constitutions confirmed the official position of French but allowed that in the future a law might permit the use of Creole "to safeguard the material and moral interests of Citizens who do not know the French language well enough" (Art. 35). Changes in the constitution in 1983 declared both French and Creole to be "national languages" and symbols of the country, but French is official or the language of administration, law, and education (Art. 62). Although Dr. Duvalier did not allow Creole in the primary schools, he did create an adult literacy service, the Office National d'Alphabétisation et d'Action Communautaire (ONAAC) which used it. Fearful that enthusiastic teachers and community organizers might succeed in mobilizing the masses—even inadvertantly—the president did not allow ONAAC to flourish. A very limited budget has constrained the Office's activities, but it contributed significantly to the development of a standard orthography and to giving the language symbolic legitimacy.

Inevitably the promotion of Creole is identified with the interests of the lowest strata while use of French is identified with the interests of the government and rich urban elites and middle classes. In a special issue of *Sel,* a newspaper published in New York, authors wrote that throughout Haitian history the French language has served the elite as a weapon to dominate the masses, and thus "The battle for Creole is, politically speaking, a battle for the liberation of the oppressed classes."[39]

Very few Haitians support Creole as the only language of instruction, however. Almost unanimously they believe in the desirability of French as the medium of instruction in the higher grades of primary school, secondary schools, and university. Bilingualism seems to be the answer. Experiments by Haitian scholars and research centers provide data supporting this bilingual policy. In the mid-1970s the Centre Haïtien d'Investigation en Sciences Sociales (CHISS), under the direction of Haitian sociologist Hubert de Ronceray, conducted experiments at Léogane which, although incomplete, provided some positive results on Creole. In the last few years Yves Joseph, currently at the important Institute Pédagogique National, found that children feel strong loyalty to Creole and believe it is useful in their day to day interactions. At the same time, they want to know French to communicate with the outside world and to enjoy successful careers.[40]

A debate over Creole spelling added another political dimension. Those who favored a phonetic spelling—one symbol for one sound introduced by U.S. scholars but modified by Haitians—were called anti-French and pro-American because the system might make learning French more difficult. Those favoring a spelling closer to French orthography were accused of promoting French interests.

While the debate intensified, Creole spread unannounced into the spoken and written media, the churches, creative works, and even into the schools without government approval. For years some Catholic and Protestant schools have been using Creole as a spoken and written means of instruction because teachers concluded French would alienate and discourage the youngest pupils. Catholic and Protestant churches print magazines in Creole, and their combined circulation may now be 50,000. Haiti's seven major radio stations, both government and private, use Creole extensively. It is obvious to the visitor to government offices, businesses, and elite social gatherings that, unlike the rest of the French- or English-speaking Caribbean, black and brown civil servants, professionals, and business people speak Creole among themselves for both personal and official purposes even though their written work is exclusively in French or English. This constant use has helped a standard form to emerge, based on Port-au-Prince Creole.

Important to the continuing expansion and development of Creole is the creative writer. The greatest names in Haiti's literary history wrote in French, but contemporary poets, novelists, playwrights, and journalists use Creole in Haiti and in exile. For many years Felix Morrisseau-Leroy has written or translated literary works into Creole. Younger writers such as Rassoul Labuchin and Franck Etienne have joined him. In 1975 Etienne wrote what is now called the first Creole novel, the highly regarded *Dezafi*. This book marks an important point in Creole history because, as Valdman points out, the author showed how the creative person can enrich the language without borrowing excessively from French or English. More important, in the view of Jean Dominique, was Franck Etienne's play *Pèlin Tèt*. In the course of about a year and a half in 1978–79 this Creole play was presented about 50 times to packed houses in the Rex Theater located in midtown Port-au-Prince. The enthusiasm of the audiences and the very indirect references to politics led the government to forbid further presentations after March 1979.[41]

In an interview with the German linguist, Ulrich Fleischmann, Franck Etienne admitted limitations on use of Creole for the time being. Because Creole is intimately tied with Haitian realities, certain abstract notions foreign to Haitian experience, are, as yet, difficult to express in Creole. He suggested that through translation, a traditional way of developing a language, and through original works the gaps can be filled by Haitian writers using their mother tongue with a concern for development and esthetics:

"When one uses this language, masks fall off. Naked reality appears; it surges forth. And you, to accept this reality, you must be naked, but with what I could call the esthetic sense. In that sense there is much to do for the writers who use Creole."[42] Exiles employ Creole or at least some Creole in their publications. *Haïti-Observateur,* published in New York, has a regular column in Creole. Bilingual programs in New York state for Haitian children use Creole rather than French, and teachers and educationists such as Yves Dejean follow linguistic developments in Haiti so that the standard is maintained in Haiti and abroad.[43]

Participants in a conference during the month of August 1979 in Port-au-Prince debated these subjects. USAID, the Institut Pédagogique National aided by the French, Indiana University, and the Haitian Department of National Education were the sponsors. At the beginning of the session the minister, Joseph C. Bernard, announced that the government had decided to allow the use of Creole as a medium of instruction. The goal of Creole instruction would be: "relief from an old injustice perpetrated against 90 percent of the population which has been kept in ignorance and illiteracy."[44] One month later the president signed a law which recognized the importance of Creole as a symbol of Haitian culture and an instrument of education:

> Article 1. The use of Creole, as a shared language spoken by 90 percent of the Haitian population, is permitted in the schools as a medium of instruction and as a subject of instruction.

He thus opened a four-year period of experimentation supported financially by the World Bank. The law also settled the problem of spelling, at least for now:

> Article 3. The Department of National Education will send to the schools the instructions with respect to the alphabet, spelling . . . and finally any sign which the specialists of this Ministry judge to be the most widespread and convenient for the standardization of Creole writing and for the teaching of this language.[45]

Another law reorganized the Department of National Education beginning a general reform of public education. In February 1982, under the continuing leadership of J.C. Bernard, the Department issued a brochure explaining a series of reforms so that schools might respond to the needs of the majority and serve development goals.[46] Experiments began with about 1,000 pupils studying newly prepared material in Creole. The children studied all subjects in Creole during their first four years of primary school. They also began to learn French as a subject. Teachers no longer assumed pupil competence in French. The first and second year they concentrated on how to speak French, and the third and fourth year they began to read and write French, so that in the fifth year they could accept French as the medium of instruction. The policy marked a sharp change and promised a radical alteration in education.

Valdman predicted opposition would harden because Creole expansion would pose a threat to the urban elite which is literate in French: "the extension of Creole into any new era of activity represents the loss of privilege for the bilingual elite since the simple fact of its fluency in French no longer ensures it will have the exclusive control of this activity."[47] Even though the reforms did not touch the Duvalier interests directly, the ruling family wants to ensure the loyalty of the urban elites and rural middlemen and women. Pressures from these elements forced Duvalier to stop the Creole program in June and July 1982, which points to a significant difference between François, who had terrorized the Port-au-Prince middle classes, and Jean-Claude, who wants their support. The president dismissed the talented minister of education and withdrew his support for the Creole program, at least for the time being.

CHURCH AND STATE

A major promoter of Creole has been the church. The Catholic church in particular has played an important role in Haitian society since colonial days. Before independence everyone was officially a Roman Catholic. The French king ordered baptism of slaves into the church. After independence the priests left, and Voodoo swept the countryside while the elites remained nominally Catholic. In 1860 Haiti and the Vatican signed a Concordat reestablishing Catholicism as the state religion. In this agreement, which is the basis for the relationship today, the Haitian government pledged to pay clergy out of public funds. The 1981–82 budget allocated more than $400,000 to pay the Catholic clergy, who number about 150 priests in 132 parishes. There are over 600 nuns and brothers, and French historian Cornevin reports there are 20,000 students in Roman Catholic educational institutions.[48]

Black peasants must have perceived the Catholic church as part of the ruling establishment because the white dominated clergy and mulatto dominated governments prior to Estimé and Duvalier often worked together to oppose Voodoo. In the early 1940s President Elie Lescot proposed suppressing Voodoo once and for all. During the subsequent anti-Voodoo campaign Alfred Métraux reported that in the Marbial Valley a French and a Haitian priest were assisted by the Chef de Section in their efforts to destroy sanctuaries:

> The priest's escort, headed by the *Chef de Section,* went into the house, took away any suspicious objects and . . . these self-appointed inquisitors took the opportunity of settling private scores or even of committing small thefts.[49]

Peasants had other reasons for complaint. In the course of his 1934 field work American anthropologist Melville Herskovits found that at Mirebalais, in the valley of the Artibonite River, peasants resented paying for church burials, baptisms, and marriages. Payments to Voodoo priests were much lower. In addition, the peasants were race and color conscious and resented the whites: "One of the sentiments about the Church most frequently heard during the field work, coming as it did just at the end of the American occupation was: 'The *Garde* has finally been Haitianized. Now it is the turn of the Church.' " In their famous novel *Canapé-Vert* the Marcelins make an ironic reference to foreign clergy: "He was one of those young Breton ecclesiasts that are manufactured in series at the seminary of Saint-Jacques for the evangelization of the Negro masses in Haiti."[50] Haitianization took a leap forward under François Duvalier after a stormy battle between the president and the church hierarchy.

Despite the alliances between church and state, the influence of the Roman Catholic church has long troubled authorities as it still does today. Since priests have controlled many of the best Port-au-Prince schools, they are in a particularly good position to encourage certain political beliefs and actions among middle-class children and adolescents. During the U.S. occupation, which sealed the steady decline in French economic and political influence in Haiti, the French-run Roman Catholic schools became centers of opposition to U.S. policy. American authorities suspected that French priests actively encouraged their students to pour into the streets in 1929 to join demonstrations which helped bring about an end to the occupation. Americans may have tried to get their revenge a decade later when the very pro-American President Elie Lescot proposed replacing French priests with American priests.

Like the peasants, the black intellectuals complained that all the bishops and the archbishops of Port-au-Prince were white. Activists in the intellectual movements reviving black and African consciousness took offense at Rome's slowness in naming black priests to high positions. In 1949 François Duvalier, then a minister in Dumarsais Estimé's government, asked church authorities to move in this direction. The following year the government was overthrown, and Duvalier, who always claimed to be a protégé of the black president, wrote that the church hierarchy had played a role in the military coup.[51] Duvalier also believed that the Catholic hierarchy favored one of his opponents in the 1957 elections.

Despite apprehensions and suspicions Duvalier invited the Jesuits to establish themselves in Haiti in 1958, offering to pay their travel expenses to the island. According to his memoirs, by 1960 Duvalier suspected the Jesuits of taking a stand against him in their schools. Student strikes that year raised his suspicions. Shortly afterward in 1961 he expelled the archbishop of Port-au-Prince as well as the bishop of Gonaïves. The French ambassador signaled his country's political protest by accompanying the archbishop to the airport. By 1964 Dr. Duvalier was convinced the Jesuits presented a major threat, and he expelled the order. During this time Duvalier was both excommunicated by the Catholic church and cut off from U.S. aid by President Kennedy's administration.

Shortly after these events negotiations opened with the Vatican to restore good relations and to Haitianize the hierarchy with politically acceptable bishops. According to the 1860 Concordat, the Haitian chief executive had the right to nominate bishops, but Rome had the right to accept or refuse.[52]

Discussions continued in Rome and Port-au-Prince during 1966.[53] The president and the Vatican finally agreed on five nominations, four bishops and one archbishop all but one of whom were black. The most important nomination was that of François Wolff Lingondé as archbishop of Port-au-Prince and the effective head of the Haitian church. Duvalier judged him politically acceptable for he was a "young and brilliant prelate from a prestigious up-country family, who had shown a high degree of national spirit during the last electoral campaign."[54] On October 25, 1966, the new church leader pledged his loyalty to the government, as required in the concordat, and he is today the highest black official in what is now a Haitianized church. From time to time since the advent of Jean-Claude Duvalier that Catholic clergy have been accused of antigovernment sermons and public comments unfavorable to the regime. In 1982 and 1983 some foreign and Haitian church personnel have become even more outspoken in their criticism of the government. The visit of Pope John Paul II to Port-au-Prince on March 9, 1983, opened a new chapter in the relations between church and state.

In his speech at Port-au-Prince airport the head of the Catholic church called for social change in Haiti and gave his blessing to priests, nuns, and lay personnel who promote change. Although most of his speech was not printed in the local press, his call, "Il faut que les choses changent" was reprinted enough to stimulate a warning from Ernest Bennett, the president's father-in-law that priests and others in the church should stay out of politics or accept the consequences.[55] Ignoring the threat, 860 priests and others signed a statement in April proposing a new dynamic role for the Roman Catholic church in Haiti: more attention to the poorest and their culture; formation of study groups and mutual aid organization in rural areas; willingness to comment publicly on national issues; discussions with other churches to find ways to help the poor; increasing the power of Christian radio stations; and a warning to the United States and Haitian governments that the priests oppose any eventual use of the Môle St-Nicolas as a U.S. base.[56] Shortly thereafter the bishops published a similar declaration. When seven of these bishops visited Rome Pope John Paul II congratulated them for the declaration and urged them to continue their efforts to improve human rights in Haiti.[57]

Numerous Protestant churches such as the Anglicans, Seventh Day Adventists, Baptists, and Mennonites account for probably 10 percent of the population. They operate schools, hospitals, printing plants, and workshops. They strive to avoid involvement in politics, although in the past Anglicans have been accused of first supporting and then opposing Dr. Duvalier. A recent exception was the Haitian Baptist pastor, Luc Nérée who published a newspaper *Jeune Presse* in 1976 and 1977. At the end of 1977 he sharply criticized the tontons macoutes in one article. After a severe beating by VSN agents he ceased publication. The Protestant churches are also active in building participatory community organizations.

POLITICAL PARTIES AND TRADE UNIONS

Other institutions such as political parties and trade unions have played a fleeting and temporary role as independent entities. Historically, since the president and legislators were elected by small cliques or the head of state seized office by military coup, political parties served no useful function. During the late nineteenth century urban mulattoes organized themselves loosely under the banner of "Liberals" while urban blacks called themselves the "Nationals," but they were not well-organized parties. During and after the U.S. occupation some parties sprang into existence, but sensing a threat from political opponents organizing against his plans to succeed himself, Dumarsais Estimé outlawed political parties in 1949. During the tumultuous months of 1956 and 1957 parties emerged around dynamic personalities including Louis Dejoie, François Duvalier, Clément Jumelle, and Daniel Fignolé, who attempted to win workers' support in his bid for the presidency. It is probably an exaggeration to call the groups of individuals around these candidates "parties." Their loyalty was to an individual rather than to an ideology, institutions or a program, and they would disappear after the elections.

Communist ideology, which attracted intellectuals such as Jacques Roumain, Jacques Stéphen Alexis, and others, provided the basis of a party which has been outlawed since Estimé's presidency. The Duvalier family has unsparingly suppressed any hint of communist activity, particularly since the advent of Fidel Castro in Cuba across the Windward Passage. Although Roumain died a natural, albeit youthful death, Alexis was killed after an abortive invasion attempt from Cuba in 1961. The Duvaliers' anti-communist law of 1969 legitimizes the death penalty for activities and organizations labeled "communist."

Nevertheless, a small Communist party has survived underground and outside Haiti. Various Marxist-Leninist factions united in 1968 to form the United Party of Haitian Communists (Parti Unifié des Communistes Haïtiens-PUCH). At the 1978 congress, secretly held within Haitian frontiers, party members demanded an end to Haitian ties with the United States and called for repeal of the anticommunist law, abolition of the presidency for life, release of political prisoners, general amnesty for political exiles, and new elections.[58]

As a result of pressure from the Carter administration, the example of the democratization process in the Dominican Republic and the urging of writers within Haiti, Jean-Claude Duvalier briefly permitted the organization of noncommunist parties in 1979. In May of that year Grégoire Eugène, a well-known professor of constitutional and civil law at the university personally published a small booklet, *Plaidoyer en faveur des partis politiques (Plea in Favor of Political Parties)*. His purpose was to show that parties are essential in a representative democracy, the modern state. In a clever analogy Professor Eugène said that Haiti could be like Spain with Jean-Claude Duvalier introducing democracy and thus modernism the way King Juan Carlos abolished the dictatorship in his country. Parties with a doctrine and organization will promote a debate "among elites;" they will work against personalization of power; and they will make Haiti into a better country. In a daring conclusion he denounced the Franquistes in Spain and the Francistes in Haiti. Perhaps this publication had some influence. In any case, the 1979 legislative elections encouraged such organizing after they were finished. Inspired by Christian Democratic and Socialist parties in Italy, where he once studied for the priesthood, Eugène founded the Haitian Social Christian Party; Sylvio Claude founded the Christian Democratic Party. A Haitian League for Human Rights, under the leadership of Lafontant Joseph, also gained adherents. Eugène's bimonthly newspaper, *Fraternité,* reached a circulation of 10,000 in 1980,[59] and he traveled north to promote his organization and ideas. Sylvio Claude published two newspapers, *Verite sou tanbou* and *La Conviction.*

The government quickly perceived these organizations as a threat and allowed the VSN to begin harassing them at the end of 1979. They were effectively suppressed at the end of 1980 by means of arrest and exile of the leaders. The anticommunist law was used to jail many party members even though they are committed to democracy, not Marxist-Leninism. Eugène was exiled to the United States, and Sylvio Claude, expelled once from the country, returned to be imprisoned. Claude was given two trials and, after pressure from the Christian Democrats of West Germany in particular, plus the French and the American Black Congressional Caucus he was released. The government then put him under a form of house arrest.

The media and other organizations were treated in similar fashion. On November 28, 1980, the police and VSN entered the offices of the Radio Haiti-Inter station. They arrested Michèle Montas, wife of popular station owner and journalist Jean Dominique, 30 employees, and others. After a few days some were freed while some were expelled from the country. Dominique had gone into hiding and then sought asylum at the Venezuelan embassy. In January he was allowed to leave the country for New York.[60]

The only approved political organization resembling a party is the Action Jean-claudiste or CONAJEC (Conseil National d'Action Jean-claudiste), with an office in Port-au-Prince. Occasional statements support the economic modernization which the president has promised. Aside from dedication to the person of the head of state and whatever he says and does, the organization seems to have no raison d'être.

Attempts to build independent trade unions have met the same fate as political parties. In 1980 workers set up 24 unions united in a confederation, the Centrale Autonome des Travailleurs Haïtiens (CATH), but the VSN and others attacked these organizations' leaders. Yves-Antoine Richard, secretary general of the confederation, was expelled along with the journalists in 1980. Occasional but brief strikes are repressed. The only exception to the restrictions on union activity is the Syndicat des Chauffeurs-Guides, the taxi drivers' union, which is thriving. Its impressive headquarters along the seaside in Port-au-Prince is a clear sign of government support. This union has been allied with the Duvalier family for decades. Dr. Duvalier ran this union prior to being elected president, and it is often alleged that he drew his first recruits to the tontons macoutes from its members.

THE MEDIA

Newspapers and radio stations are important institutions, but they are watched and increasingly monitored. One television station, Télévision Nationale d'Haïti, is government-owned and operated The other, Télé-Haïti, is privately owned. There are four daily newspapers one of which, *Le Nouveau Monde,* is government-owned. The privately held *Le Matin* has the largest circulation, 10,000, compared with only 7,500 for *Le Nouveau Monde,* 5,500 for *Le Nouvelliste,* and 2,000 for *Panorama.* The total circulation of all dailies is thus 25,000,[61] an indication that these publications have little influence. Another sign is that they are very difficult to find since few people other than civil servants, diplomats, and a few business people read them. A law passed in September 1979, and tightened the following March, gives the government the power to censor all publications before distribution, to limit journalists' freedom by requiring a special identity card to practice their profession, to hold booksellers responsible for any material on their shelves, and to threaten journalists with imprisonment from one to three years for any statement interpreted to be an insult to the head of state or to his wife.[62]

A weekly newspaper, *Le Petit Samedi Soir,* with a circulation of 11,000, the highest in the country, has often printed articles at least indirectly critical of the government, and one of its journalists was murdered after he wrote a story about a strike at a cement factory in 1976. The owner-publisher is able to point out negative features of the regime but is not allowed to criticize the important political and business families. It is surprising how far this publication and others could go in criticizing conditions in Haiti until 1980. In her study Carolyn Fowler found 13 independent newspapers and magazines in the capital. *Le Fil d'Ariane, Inter-Jeunes, Regard, Coquerico,* and others challenged President Jean-Claude Duvalier to live up to his promises of democratization.[63] Like Mao's "Let a Hundred Flowers Bloom" campaign in China in 1957, the Haitian government occasionally tolerates minor criticisms in publications of limited circulation. It uses these outbursts in print to identify potential opposition circles, and to provide outlets for grievances. In 1979 *Le Petit*

Samedi Soir published an opinion poll showing that most people feel insecure, not a flattering result for the government.

However, under Jean-Claude Duvalier, unlike under François Duvalier, foreign journalists are extraordinarily free to investigate foreign aid projects, emigration, and local life; American lawyers denouncing human rights violations come and go; U.S. congressional delegations visit the prisons and give press conferences. Foreign scholars who have condemned the regime in articles and books are allowed in. This regime is much less concerned with foreign views of Haiti than with controlling the Haitian media.

As in most countries with a low rate of literacy, the radio, rather than newspapers, has been the major source of news and daily entertainment. The impression one gains from traveling about the country is that rural people with access to a radio listen to the news and comments very carefully and are now informed better than ever before. Radio Cacique, broadcasting in French and Creole, provided Sylvio Claude with a means to disseminate his ideas. Radio Haïti-Inter, owned by Jean Dominique, had perhaps the most influence. It exposed a plan to dump nuclear waste from North America in Haiti, forcing the government to cancel the project. Haitians followed carefully the commentaries and news delivered by Jean Dominique and Michèle Montas.[64] By November 1980 most independent Haitian press and radio journalists were silenced, but Gérard Duclerville, a Catholic lay worker, continued to give voice to some criticisms of official policy. His arrest in 1983, alleged torture, and eventual release just before the Pope's visit angered and helped unify Catholics critical of the regime.

INTEREST GROUPS

Lastly, we should note the existence of four organizations of business and manufacturing interests. The Association of Exporters of Coffee (ASDEC) was first established during the regime of Dr. Duvalier partly as a defense against him. The president wished to weaken the white and mulatto families in Port-au-Prince who controlled coffee exports. In Girault's view, the ASDEC provides a framework for agreements among the exporters about price, relations with the government, and wages to be paid. It facilitates the existence of a cartel.[65]

The second organization is the Haitian American Chamber of Commerce and Industry (Hamcham), which, as the name suggests, articulates the interests of major businesses, promotes sales of Haitian goods in the United States, and helps Americans who wish to do business in Haiti. It has been more active in recent years than the older Haitian Chamber of Commerce which includes traditional retail and wholesale businesses and favors conservative economic policies.

The fourth and most interesting organization is the Haitian Manufacturers Association (ADIH) with headquarters in the growing area of Delmas between Port-au-Prince and Pétionville. The members are the owners and managers of assembly industries and other growing enterprises. They represent a new generation of mainly brown-skinned, English-speaking entrepreneurs quite different from the the old coffee, sugar, and hotel interests. They wish to modernize the country's industrial establishment, rationalize labor practices and relations with the government, and, of course, maximize profits. Many have been educated in the United States, where they have friends and relatives; they travel to Miami, San Juan, New York, and Paris with ease and know the latest technological developments in their industry. They socialize among themselves and have no contact with rural Haiti and only limited contacts with older business sectors.

All this means that there are very few institutions in Haiti's first world. Beneath a placid exterior and appearance of order are shifting alliances and tense relationships around the fount of legitimacy and power, Jean-Claude Duvalier. But the president, concerned with his security and prosperity, cannot directly control the countryside or all the ministries. Unlike his father he is too young to have the personal relationships; nor does he have a well-articulated ideology. His marriage to very fair-skinned Michele Bennett partially negated black power ideas and linked him to the Bennett family business interests which include coffee. (His father-in-law, Ernest Bennett, has reportedly become the largest exporter of coffee since the marriage.) He will naturally act to protect these interests.

Like most of his predecessors, President Duvalier must ensure that the most effective organizations are those concerned with taxing and policing. Order is the watchword; political stagnation and oppression are the results. Under pressure from outside, reforms are undertaken, as are steps toward political participation, but at the first sign of threat the reforms are reversed or nullified in some way which may not be immediately evident to the outside observer. A growing weakness in the system is the massive corruption at the center, nothing new, but dangerous in a context of a decline in agriculture which contributes to a disaggregation of the rural world. Extraction of money to pay the holders of what we have called "the franchise" is increasingly difficult.

If the Duvaliers fail to provide funds or the means to obtain funds for the intermediaries on whom the system depends, the support of the VSN, the Chefs de Section, the army, and civil servants will weaken. If local rulers or administrators perceive that loyalty to the Duvalier family no longer provides them with money and personal security, they will be willing to follow other claimants to power in Port-au-Prince.

NOTES

1. Paul Moral, *Le paysan haïtien* (1961, reprint ed., Port-au-Prince, Fardin, 1978), pp. 53–54.

2. Some of the information concerning the early constitutions from James G. Leyburn, *The Haitian People* (1941; reprint ed. New Haven: Yale University Press, 1966), pp. 238–49.

3. Hans Schmidt, *The United States Occupation of Haiti 1915–1934* (New Brunswick, New Jersey, Rutgers University Press, 1971), p. 100.

4. *Constitution de la République d'Haïti,* 1964 Amendée (Port-au-Prince, Presses Nationales d'Haïti, *1971). For the 1983 changes see Haïti-Observateur,* 9–16 Sept., 1983, pp. 9–12.

5. Michael Hooper, mimeographed, "Violations of Human Rights in Haiti: A Report of the Lawyers Committee for International Human Rights to the Organization of American States," November 1980, p. 5.

6. *Constitution.*

7. Ibid.

8. Kern Delince, *Armée et politique en Haïti* (Paris: Editions L'Harmattan, 1979), pp. 66–70.

9. "Regime's Candidate Loses in Haiti Vote," in *New York Times,* 17 May 1983, p. 3.

10. Jean-Claude García-Zamor, *La Adminstración Publica en Haiti,* (Guatemala: Editorial Landivar, 1966), pp. 82–83.

11. Pnina Lahav, "The Chef de Section: Structures and Functions of Haiti's Basic Administrative Institution," in *Working Papers in Haitian Society and Culture* (ed. Sidney W. Mintz, New Haven: Yale University Antilles Research Program, 1975), pp. 60–61. See also Jean L. Comhaire, "The Haitian 'Chef de Section,' " *American Anthropologist* 57 (1955): 620–623.

12. Leyburn, *The Haitian People,* p. 247.

13. Docteur François Duvalier, *Mémoires d'un leader du Tiers Monde* (Paris, Hachette, 1969) p. 318.

14. Christian A. Girault, *Le commerce du café en Haïti: Habitants, spéculateurs et exportateurs* (Paris: CNRS, 1981), p. 236.

15. Georges Anglade, *Espace et liberté en Haïti* (Montreal: ERCE and CRC, 1982), p. 65–67. Some of his data come from Duplan, Lagra, and Locher.

16. According to Suzy Castor, *La ocupación norteamericana de Haití y sus consecuencias (1915–1934)* (Mexico: Siglo Veintiuno, 1971), pp. 123–24.

17. Delince, *Armée et politique,* p. 88.

18. Hooper, *Violations of Human Rights,* p. 11.

19. Serge Vieux, "Research Problems and Perspectives of the Haitian Civil Service," in *The Haitian Potential: Research and Resources of Haiti,* ed. Vera Rubin and Richard P. Schaedel (New York: Teachers College Press, 1975), ftn. 12, p. 246.

20. Jean-Claude Garcia-Zamor, "Haiti," in *Latin America and Caribbean Contemporary Record* (New York: Holmes and Meier, 1983), p. 579.

21. Ibid., p. 580.

22. Ibid., p. 580.

23. "Budget Général de l'Exercise 1981–1982, Octobre 1981–September 1982," in *Le Moniteur Officiel,* vol. 1, (28 September 1981), pp. 77, 93, 95.

24. Ibid., p. 106.

25. JWK International Corporation, "Coffee Policy Study: Haiti" (Damien, Haiti: Agricultural Policy Project, on contract with AID, 15 April 1976), p. V–4.

26. Derick Brinkerhoff et al., "Administrative Reform and Plans for Decentralization in Haiti," Report for USAID (Port-au-Prince, November 1981), p. 8.

27. Garcia-Zamor, *La Administracion,* pp. 578–79.

28. See *Le Petit Samedi Soir,* 21–27 August 1982, p. 3.

29. Laënnec Hurbon, *Culture et dictature en Haïti: L'imaginaire sous contrôle* (Paris: L'Harmattan, 1979), pp. 72–73.

30. Albert Valdman, "Education Reform and the Instrumentalization of the Vernacular in Haiti" in Charles R. Foster, ed., *Issues in International Bilingual Education: The Role of the Vernacular* (New York: Plenum Press, 1982), pp. 144–45.

31. Most of the above data are from Jacomine de Regt, "Basic Education in Haiti," in Charles R. Foster, ed., *Haiti: An Interdisplinary Study* (Durham: Duke University, forthcoming), pp. 2, 7.

32. Valdman, p. 144.

33. Ibid.

34. Garcia-Zamor, "Haiti," p. 582.

35. Ibid.

36. Jean Price-Mars *La vocation de l'élite* (1919; reprint ed., Port-au-Prince, Fardin, 1976), pp. 71–72.

37. Cited by Albert Valdman, *Le Créole: Structure, statut et origine* (Paris: Klincksieck, 1978), pp. 313–14.

38. See Nadine Dutcher, *The Use of First and Second Languages in Primary Education: Selected Case Studies,* World Bank Staff Working Paper No. 504, January 1982 (Washington: World Bank, 1982).

39. "Numero Espesial sou Kreyol," *Sel* 4: (Oktobo 1972) p. 5. For a chauvinistic French view see Robert Cornevin, *Haiti* (Paris: PUF, Que sais-je? 1982), p. 105. Also see, Max Chancy, "Education et déeveloppement en Haiti," in *Culture et developpement en Haiti,* ed. Emerson (Ottawa: Editions Lemeac, 1972), pp. 135–55.

40. Yves J. Joseph, "Enquête pilote sur l'environnement linguistique de l'enfant haïtien," in *Créole et enseignement primaire en Haïti*, 2nd. ed., ed. Albert Valdman with Yves Joseph, Bloomington: Indiana University, 1980), pp. 75–94.

41. Interview with Jean Dominique, 31 May 1983.

42. Ulrich Fleischmann, "Entrevue avec Franck Etienne sur son roman 'Dezafi'," *Dérives* 7 (1977): 20–21.

43. Information from Charles R. Foster, editor of a forthcoming book on Haiti.

44. Joseph C. Bernard, "Discours du Ministre de l'Education Nationale d'Haiti," in *Créole et enseignement primaire en Haiti*, 2nd ed., ed., Albert Valdman (Bloomington: Indiana University, 1980), p. 7.

45. Law of 28 September 1979, reprinted in *Bulletin* of the Institut Pedagogique National 1 (December 1979): 13–21.

46. Departement de l'Education Nationale, *La réforme éducative: Eléments d'information* (Port-au-Prince, Institut Pédagogique Nationale, 1982).

47. Albert Valdman, "La diglossie français-créole dans l'univers plantocratique," in *Plurilinguisme: Normes, situations, stratégies*, ed. G. Manessy and Paul Weld (Paris: L'Harmattan, 1979), p. 183.

48. Cornevin, *Haiti*, p. 94.

49. Alfred Métraux, *Voodoo in Haiti*, trans. Hugo Charteris (New York: Oxford University Press, 1959), p. 346.

50. Melville J. Herskovits, *Life in a Haitian Valley* (Garden City, New York: Doubleday, 1971), p. 292. Philippe Thoby-Marcelin and Pierre Marcelin, *Canapé Vert*, trans. Edward Larocque Tinker (New York: Farrar and Rinehart, 1944), p. 183.

51. Duvalier, *Mémoires*, pp. 93–94.

52. Ibid., p. 189.

53. Ibid., p. 229.

54. One journal that did print the Pope's slogan was *Jonction* 20 (17 March 1983):9. For the Bennett replies see *Le Petit Samedi Soir*, 26 March–1 April 1983, pp. 12–13. And *Haïti-Observateur*, 25 March–1 April 1983, p. 16. For an American view of the Pope's visit see Edward Cody, "Pontiff, in Haiti, Pleads for Social Justice, Rights," in *Washington Post*, 10 March 1983, p. 1.

55. Reproduced in *Haïti-Observateur*, 6–13 May 1983, p. 2. The bishops also issued a statement affirming the activist role of the church.

56. "Pope Backs 7 Bishops from Haiti on Rights," in *New York Times* 12 June 1983, p. 5.

57. Lynn Ratliff, "Haiti," in *Yearbook on International Communist Affairs 1979*, ed. Richard F. Staar (Stanford: Hoover Institution Press, 1979), pp. 359–60.

58. Interview with Professor Eugène, 14 January 1983.

59. Interview with Jean Dominique, 31 May 1983.

60. See *Le Monde*, 12 February 1981, p. 3.

61. Circulation data from Jean-Claude Garcia-Zamor, ''Haiti,'' pp. 582–83.

62. See *Le Moniteur: Journal Officiel de la République d'Haïti*, 3 April 1980, pp. 231–33.

63. Carolyn Fowler, ''The Emergence of the Independent Press in Haiti: Background to Repression,'' in *The Black Collegian* (April–May 1981): 149–51.

64. Ibid., p. 151.

65. Girault, *Le commerce du cáfe*, p. 217.

4

THE ECONOMY:
COFFEE AND BASEBALLS

The money to rule Haiti is extracted from the poor and solicited from foreign donors. Unlike the political families in many other countries, Haitian leaders have had few independent sources of very large income from the land, mines, or industry. In contrast with much of Latin America and Asia, there are no great estates or latifundia although there are some individual land holdings large by Haitian standards. Nor is there slavery, covert or overt, or widespread coerced labor to produce wealth for the few in Haiti.

As a result, control of the government and bureaucracy, which can extract resources from the producers, consumers, and foreigners, is the major source of wealth. Since President Pétion, monopoly over government ensures a flow of money in favor of urban elites through the fiscal system, as Mats Lundahl has explained.[1] A wide range of indirect taxes, imposed after independence in the form of export and import duties, are paid by the peasant coffee producers and workers in baseball and other assembly plants; and this ensures a steady redistribution of income toward Port-au-Prince where the government spends most of the money received. Direct taxes on incomes, corporate profits, and property are very low, and they are collected irregularly.

More precisely, the fiscal system operates in such a way that the 80 percent rural population pays about 85 percent of Haitian government internally generated revenues while receiving less than 20 percent of government expenditures in return.[2] The $400 million annual budget of 1981–82 allocated 80 percent of expenditures to salaries and fringe benefits for urban-based personnel. The failure to appropriate funds for overhead, maintenance, and operations means that many government offices have salaried staff and little else.

The fiscal system also distorts income distribution. Foreign economists estimate that 8,000 families representing 1 percent of the population have an average annual income in excess of $54,000, concentrate about 44 percent of the national income, and are obliged to pay a tiny 3.5 percent of their revenues in direct taxes. Grégoire Eugène believes there are 200 millionaires in the country.[3] Perennially starved for savings, Haiti's tax generosity toward these families results mostly in their consumption of imported luxury goods at low tariffs or in investment abroad.

The ruling families are wealthy by Haitian but not by global super-rich standards. Former President Magloire paved his exile with investments abroad, as his predecessors had done, but the holdings of the Duvalier family have broken all previous records. Money is funneled to them through the Régie du Tabac, through their extensive private holdings, and by siphoning off other public funds, kickbacks on contracts, and other means. It is impossible to know the size of the Duvalier fortune, but if the guesses of $200 million are correct, their holdings seem small compared with the reputed wealth of Mobutu in Zaire, the late Shah of Iran, or the Somozas of Nicaragua. Their life style is also less flamboyant. For instance the Duvaliers rarely travel abroad, and avoid ostentation. Yet their wealth is enormous in the context of Haitian poverty.

The wealthy also benefit from ridiculously low direct taxes. In 1979 revenue from personal income taxes was less than $3 million; corporate income taxes brought in less than $13 million; and property taxes only $540,000. Excise taxes on flour, sugar, cigarettes, and petroleum products were about equal in revenue to corporate income taxes.[4] The Régie du Tabac collects many of these highly regressive excise taxes which severely burden the poor.

Haiti's development efforts are part of a separate budget of which foreign aid provides at least 80 percent. The Budget for Development, 1981–82, totaled 981,566,763 gourdes or almost $250 million. The government pledged to contribute about 290 million gourdes or $58 million,[5] but observers doubt the government is able to contribute this much. Furthermore, as a sign of the lack of involvement of the central government, an observer reported that the Ministry of Planning was ignorant of investment projects being planned in one recent budget.

Individual aid projects have improved telecommunications; they have paved and maintained major and minor roads, introduced family planning, organized hurricane disaster relief, and provided food. For many years, almost all development projects in Haiti, successful or not, have been donor funded and initiated. The government is usually a passive observer of development efforts.

The emphasis in recent development budgets is agriculture—about $48 million or a quarter of the total. Roads come next with 18.7 percent and then community development at 9.7 percent. Health was to receive 8.9 percent and education 8.3 percent. The emphasis on agriculture reflects the fact that this sector has always been the most important part of the Haitian economy, as well as the most neglected.

AGRICULTURE

The roots of this economy lie in the immediate postindependence period. While Henri Christophe in the kingdom of the north relied on coerced labor to reestablish abandoned estates for the production and export of sugar, coffee, and indigo, Alexandre Pétion in the south distributed land. As early as 1840 the pattern had spread nationally of de facto and de jure small farms, reinforced by inheritance providing land for legitimate and illegitimate children. It is important to note, however, that while small holdings are the rule the government can claim to control all lands for which current occupants have no proof of ownership as well as all abandoned lands. This makes the government the largest landholder, but it does not exercise its option over much of this land. It appears that a very high mortality rate and favorable export prices and high productivity kept argicultural output slightly ahead of population increase to about 1930 with many pronounced ups and downs. Little of this slight longterm growth trickled down to the peasants although during the U.S. occupation they did benefit temporarily from improved roads and schools. The Depression was a period of severe austerity followed by the relative boom years of 1940 to 1954 spurred by high world prices for coffee, military aid, and then economic or development aid, and the beginnings of large-scale tourism and export industries. The effects were felt mainly in Port-au-Prince.

As Table 4.1 shows, agriculture is still the most important sector in the national economy constituting in 1979 about 40 percent of Gross

TABLE 4.1:
Gross Domestic Product by Sector, 1965–79
(million of 1955 Gourdes)

	1965	1970	1975	1976	1977	1978	1979	Average Annual Growth (%)	
								1960–70	1970–79
Agriculture	755.7	698.9	809.6	849.3	823.7	887.7	869.9	–0.7	2.5
Mining and Quarrying	22.5	28.6	23.6	32.2	30.9	28.7	28.7	5.0	0.0
Manufacturing	161.5	163.8	206.3	250.7	268.4	269.5	291.1	0.6	6.6
Construction	29.0	36.8	82.4	92.2	98.2	110.3	119.1	1.8	13.9
Public Utilities	19.0	21.6	39.1	48.3	49.9	45.6	47.0	3.9	9.0
Transport and Communications	57.8	56.8	49.2	55.1	68.3	80.0	85.0	0.0	4.8
Commerce	165.4	164.1	193.0	223.5	227.6	238.4	245.5	–0.6	4.6
Banking and Insurance	13.4	7.5	12.3	15.2	17.0	17.4	17.0	–4.2	9.5
Housing	144.9	156.8	169.8	173.0	176.0	180.0	182.0	1.6	1.7
Government	101.8	122.2	148.8	142.1	145.2	150.0	155.0	2.2	2.7
Personal Services	102.8	103.6	123.9	132.8	135.0	142.1	147.0	1.8	4.0
GDP at Market Prices	1,573.8	1,560.7	1,858.1	2,014.4	2,040.3	2,148.8	2,187.3	0.2	3.8

Source: IBRD Current Economic Position and Prospects of Haiti, 1978, Institut Haitien de Statistique, and mission estimates.

Domestic Product. The data also show that over the long run agriculture is stagnant although average annual growth was positive from 1970–79 as compared with negative growth during François Duvalier's rule from 1960 to 1970. Every sector of the Haitian economy except for mining grew more from 1970 to 1979 than during the François Duvalier years. Construction, banking, and insurance, public utilities, and manufacturing grew from 6.6 percent to 13.9 percent whereas they were stagnant or declined from 1960 to 1970. Part of the reason is the return to Haiti of Haitian entrepreneurs and technicians during the first years of Jean-Claude Duvalier's rule; another reason is the increase in foreign assistance over the last decade. Although manufacturing has continued to grow since 1979, agriculture has faltered and declined slightly in the 1980s.

A delicate balancing mechanism worked in the past to keep the rural economy operating. Unlike frequent images of Third World peasants, the Haitian "habitants" are not subsistence farmers. They do not feed themselves entirely from their own production. They raise industrial and food crops and animals; they produce charcoal to sell for cash with which they purchase food and materials. The previously mentioned Madame Sarahs buy the surplus food production for cash and resell it to women retailers. This network succeeds in supplying rural and particularly urban markets. The need for cash combines with climatic and soil profiles to favor food cultivation for domestic markets, and coffee or other products for domestic markets and export. There is some freedom of choice: if indirect taxes are too high on industrial crops, discouraged farmers will cut back on export crops, even uprooting coffee trees to replace them with food crops. Since the Haitian government is unable to influence the world prices of any product, it is constrained to find a level of tax that will not overly discourage producers while providing the government and the ruling elites with essential revenues.

There is no typical Haitian peasant or "habitant," but it is possible to draw a composite.[6] They are Creole-speaking only, illiterate, and black. Like nine out of ten of their neighbors, they live in the same section where they were born and raised. Landholdings add up to slightly more than three acres; in much of the country they are separated into five or more scattered plots some of which are now on steep hillsides. They also have a garden next to their home. They probably lack written proof of tenure, but title is based on historical recollections and the vital fact that their ancestors are buried on this land. Both male and female self-assurance, sense of belonging, and dignity seem to belie their poverty and the stagnation of the rural economy, but they must be ready to fight for their land against the efforts of VSN landowners and merchants to increase their own holdings at peasants' expense. Christian Girault warns observers not to forget there are also "tens of thousands" of landless laborers and peasants. This is not a large percentage of a rural population of more than four million,[7] but Anglade predicts the appearance of large plantations and "the disappearance of the peasantry,"[8] if the process of consolidation, expulsion, and purchase of land continues. The laborers are hired by more prosperous peasants owning six or more acres, whereas the average farmer relies on the extended family for unpaid labor, plus the occasional and informal reciprocal services of neighbors.

The farmers' tools are the machete and the hoe. Mechanization is far too expensive and unsuitable for the fragmented, steep, and eroded plots. Attempts to introduce improved nonmechanical technologies such as ox-drawn ploughs and harnesses have faltered due to costs, distribution, and lack of credit, but they succeeded in flatter areas around Hinche. Credit is the key problem for the smallest landholder as it is only available on short terms and at usurious interest rates from middlemen and women and traders. The latter get credit on easier terms from exporters in Port-au-Prince. Access to credit is a sign of class difference in rural areas.

Female and male Haitian peasants are fiercely individualistic and independent and generally belong to no economic organization. Recently, private voluntary organizations using money from United States AID have experimented with loans of about $1,000 to groups of peasants who, according to reports, work well together.[9] Haitian intellectuals have long proposed the production cooperative as one way to strenghten the rural economy and improve peasant relationships with each other. The characters in *Récolte,* a novel by the well-known author Félix Morisseau-Leroy, discuss cooperatives.[10] Marketing cooperatives have been tried with mixed results. The commitment to private individual trading is strong, and, more important, exporters have apparently complained about cooperatives and credit programs for peasants because they see their interests adversely affected by greater peasant liberty. Some Haitians believe that pressure from Port-au-Prince exporters has prevented government and foreign support for cooperatives.

Farmers are wholly dependent on their resources for information and instruction. There are no regular visits from agricultural extension officers with advice based on research into Haitian agriculture. Understandably, the cultivators turn to their favorite spirits for aid and advice. If they favor him and her, they may also keep a few goats, pigs, poultry, and even a cow, all of which graze on land which should be lying fallow.

Rather than seeing government support, the rural "habitants" wish only not to be bothered by rapacious soldiers, usurers, Chefs de Section, and tontons macoutes who often enough covet the peasants' meager resources. Thus, the rural dweller is divided whether improved rural roads would make it easier for the state to get at him or for him to get the coffee and food to market.

We must add to this discussion that women play a special and highly independent role in rural Haiti. They are responsible for almost all farm to market transport and actual marketing of food and cash crops. Women will walk with the produce on their heads or, if fortunate, guide or ride a donkey to the nearest rural crossroads. Some will go on to one of the 550 agricultural market places in the countryside.[11] Women engaged in petty trade are also the principal users of the ubiquitous "tap taps" or gaily decorated passenger and freight trucks of Haiti to carry them and their merchandise further along.

Women are full participants in cultivation and harvest. They have full inheritance rights and usually retain a small plot and a garden. From agricultural production and trade they have a source of income. Many are completely independent from men: they maintain their own households, raise their children by themselves, and take part in Voodoo at all levels from acolytes to priestesses. Female-male relationships in Haiti are the subject of much humor, and many proverbs and sayings.

If the peasants live in the hills, they may rely on coffee trees for their principal cash income. If not, they depend on sisal, sugar, vetiver oil, cacao, and citrus fruits. Even the coffee growers spend more of their time on food crops which are for home consumption and sale for cash. Their wish is to join that 12 percent of all Haitian farmers who have eight acres or more of quality land and use it to produce two-thirds of all good and export crops. Their chances are poor though of becoming a "gros neg" (or important person) as the more prosperous habitants are called. They are forever held back by poor and eroded land, lack of irrigation or credit, ignorance, and disease. Their household income from farming may be a meager $60 a year compared to $300 for the fortunate few.[12]

Their methods of cultivation maximize return in the short run but exhaust the soil in the long run because they do not let the land rest and encourage erosion by removing trees, their only source of fuel. They cultivate vertically starting below ground with roots and tubercules such as potatoes, manioc, and yams. At ground level there are watermelons, tomatoes, and other vine crops and a little higher is cotton. Five feet above ground one finds corn, sorghum, and sugar cane, near the coffee, cacao.

Twenty feet above the ground or higher are the fruit trees such as avocados and mangos, and above them the lianas and other fibers used for rope-making, thatching, and other purposes such as making hats and baskets for sale. Sisal and cactus are used for enclosures.[13]

This system has its own delicate equilibrium which can be upset by too much or too little rain, natural disasters such as hurricanes, and an end-less number of human disasters and disputes. It does not provide an ade-quate diet for children, adults, or domesticated animals because it is heavy in starches and short in proteins. It has been estimated that the average Haitian consumes 86.4 percent of the daily required calories, but much of this comes from sugar cane or at certain times of the year mangoes.[14] These products fill the stomach and raise the calorie intake, but they nourish neither brain nor muscles. The undernourished children of the land cannot become strong and vigorous adults.

The Haitian habitant understands the ravages of erosion and deforesta-tion. As an individual there is little he or she can do to repair the damage, however. Even joined with a few neighbors there are limits to the trees which can be replanted, although anthropologist Gerald Murray, work-ing with United States AID money allocated to the Pan American Develop-ment Foundation, has introduced fast growing and lightweight tree seed-lings into selected rural areas in an effort to stop erosion and to provide a source of income. A new type of business, agroforestry, may, in Mur-ray's view, raise the standard of living and save the soil.[15] However, there are serious limits to such efforts: soil antierosion programs and refor-estation required national efforts and these have been wanting in a govern-ment whose sole 1981 budget increases were for the tourism, information, and interior ministries.

COFFEE

Coffee survived the breakup of the colonial estates because, unlike sugar, it can grow in the hills and does not require large tracts of land, annual planting, or constant care. In his study of the Haitian peasant French geographer Paul Moral used the pejorative term "grappillage" which he took from the peasants themselves to describe coffee and agriculture tech-niques. An untranslatable term, it is a form of activity midway between cultivation and collection; it is small scale, primitive, and destructive because ignorant and enslaved to the vagaries of the weather.[16] No other economically productive activity engages so many people as coffee "grap-pillage." Geographer Christian Girault estimates that there are "180,000 coffee producers representing a family population of about 900,000 persons.''[17]

Haitian coffee exports have steadily declined from 35,000 tons per year a century ago to 19,700 tons per year in the late 1970s. Since Haitians are great coffee drinkers, they consume another 15,000 tons per year, but overall rates of production are only 266.5 kilograms per hectare, the lowest in the hemisphere.[18]

The most important reason for the decline and low productivity is government indifference. Coffee producers are left to themselves, and they do the minimum to take care of their trees: Girault reports that trees must regenerate themselves because old trees are not replaced with young ones; they are not pruned; they receive no fertilizer; peasants regularly pull coffee berries from branches in such a way that damage is done to the trees. The government Coffee Institute (Institut Haïtien de Promotion de Café et des Denrées d'Exportation or I.H.P.C.A.D.E.) is supposed to control coffee production and transport, and to enforce the Coffee Code, but it does not. The fact that peasant landholdings are dispersed in very small plots adds to the inefficiency and wastage: 15 percent of coffee plots are less than 0.6 hectares in size; 19.4 percent are from 0.6 to 1.3; the largest number or 30.6 percent are from 1.3 to 2.6 hectares with 23.9 percent from 2.6 to 6.0. Only 11.1 percent of all coffee plantations are more than 6.0 hectares in area.[19]

Peasants harvest the coffee beginning in September, and they sell it to middlemen called ''spéculateurs'' who live in the small towns or ''bourgs''dotting the countryside. It is likely the middlemen are also merchants from whom the peasants have borrowed money or obtained food as a form of loan. Thus, the coffee is used to pay off indebtedness rather than as a source of new income. Both producers and middlemen are Haitian, generally black, of rural origin and residence. Unlike the producer, the middleman knows some French in addition to Creole which permits him to deal with exporters and other city people as well as the peasants.

Although middlemen are part of the second world, they try to accumulate enough wealth to send their children to private schools in Port-au-Prince and to become professionals and civil servants. They have helped build a larger black middle class in Port-au-Prince, and one Haitian scholar estimated that up to 40 percent of the personnel in the upper administration owes its origin to families engaged in agricultural speculation as well as some landholding families.[20] Although observers have accused the middlemen of exploiting the producers because of low prices, money lending practices, and absence of competition among middlemen, it does not appear they make excessive profit from buying and selling coffee. It is true the market for the sale of coffee is not as open and free as the market for food crops, but Mats Lundahl maintains that the relationship between peasant coffee producers and middlemen is not where exploitation takes place. There is competition among middlemen; the peasants find ways to counteract false weighing practices used by middlemen with their own tricks; middlemen's profits are not huge—"an average spéculateur gross profit of a mere 1.3 percent of the f.o.b. price of coffee."[21] The largest profits are made by the exporters at the end of the chain. They have the responsibility of transmitting to the government the export duties which represent a heavy tax on the producer because they are subtracted entirely before he is paid. G. Caprio has written that these internal forces and relationships are less important for an understanding of the Haitian economy than the international coffee market. Haiti's share of that market is minuscule, and it must mutely accept prices and conditions set by the United States, Brazil, Colombia, and others. Nonetheless, we believe that the relations between producer, middleman, and exporter have a dynamism of their own which affects political and economic development.[22]

Middlemen send the coffee by truck to Cap Haïtien, Jérémie, and Port-au-Prince where it is sold to one of about 27 export houses controlled, for the most part, by mulattoes and persons of European origin. In 1956–57 as in 1976–77 the three largest exporters, Madsen of Danish origin, Brandt of British and Jamaican origin, and Wiener of German origin, controlled 44.1 percent of the exports.[23] (By 1982 Bennett joined this group.)

The exporters prepare the coffee for shipment. They must sort it, remove impurities, and bag it; they arrange for shipping and sale mainly to North American and French buyers. Although they may purchase the coffee in Cap Haïtien or Jérémie, they generally ship it out of Port-au-Prince.

Exporters seem to work closely together through their association, the ASDEC, or Association des Exportateurs de Café, leading observers to conclude they maintain a cartel over purchase and sales. There is no competition "to the detriment of the producers who receive a lower price than they would otherwise have done."[24] The exporters are therefore in a position to set a price to pay the middlemen with extensive knowledge about the price they, the exporters, can expect. Because the middlemen have often borrowed money from the exporters in order to lend to the producers, there is a certain amount of dependence on the exporters. Loans are paid back with coffee. If banks lent to middlemen and producers, they would be free to negotiate or hold back their product until supplies decreased. Indebtedness eliminates possibilities for negotiation and long-term storage. If the Coffee Intitute set a fair price to be paid to producers, as it is supposed to do by law, the producer might be better protected. Since he has no independent source of finance and cannot count on government assistance, "the price obtained by the producer at the end of the chain is a residual price. The 'habitant' only receives for this product what the system wants to give him once the State and the commercial agents have taken their part."[25] In short, the exporter, who knows what he will earn from sales abroad, what he must pay women to sort the coffee, how much he must pay as an export tax to the Administration Générale des Douanes (Customs Administration), and how much he must pay for his license decides how much to pay the middleman who then knows how much to pay the producer. The producer has no control over price, and he pays the tax for everyone else along the line. The shocking result is that the coffee producer pays the highest taxes in Haiti—equivalent to an income tax of 35 to 40 percent, according to Girault and JWK International Corporation.[26]

Put another way, producers receive 43.3 to 47 percent of the price paid by the foreign purchaser with the rest—slightly more than half—going for taxes and profits plus expenses of exporter and middleman.[27] In dollar terms, the average producer made $67.10 in 1972–73 and $46.10 in 1974–75.[28]

No other country taxes coffee producers the way Haiti does. The neighboring Dominican Republic has no export tax on coffee which naturally encourages Haitians near the frontier to send coffee to Santo Domingo. The relatively low return also perpetuates poor maintenance or grappillage and a shift to food crops where there is freer trade and greater hope for a decent return.

Another unfortunate result of the pricing system is that the fixed price set in Port-au-Prince does nothing to encourage a better quality coffee. The Haitian product is rich and full-bodied, as experienced coffee drinkers know, but it could be better and more plentiful if producers were encouraged by a fairer price system and lower taxes.

In an attempt to help peasants earn more money from coffee, the United Nations and foreign missionaries have encouraged producers to establish cooperatives which could sell directly to foreign countries thereby avoiding the middlemen and exporters. Only about 1,000 producers have joined, and disputes among them have severely limited their effectiveness. Nor has the government helped them.

The government could help in other ways by strengthening the Coffee Institute. The Institute officials are supposed to have the power to make sure the peasant gets a fair return for his product, but they do not because some of them have other jobs and they engage in coffee speculation themselves. Tontons macoutes within the Institute reportedly intimidate higher ranking officials because of links with those who benefit from low prices. If peasants have trouble with the Coffee Institute for breaking or allegedly breaking the law regulating coffee harvesting, they have no guarantee of a fair trial. The official will not bring them to court but to the tontons macoutes or the army for punishment, which can be brutal and extortionist.[29]

INDUSTRY

Due primarily to low agricultural productivity, Haiti's domestic market is characterized by extremely limited purchasing power and market size. The effective market size for most products is less than that of a middle-income North American city of 50,000 persons. The result has been the evolution of two distinct kinds of industrialization: monopoly or oligopoly production for the Haitian market, and export industries lured by cheap and docile labor and generous tax incentives. Table 4.2, which groups 201 of the approximately 450 manufacturing enterprises in Port-au-Prince by numbers of employees and sectors, illustrates this division. Production of cement, essential oils, paper and printing, leather and footwear, beverages and food products is based on obsolete technologies providing often shoddy goods for local markets. The French and Haitian cement factory has a monopoly, and uses wasteful technology which consumes excessive amounts of electricity. The electronic components plants, baseball, toys, and other assembly for export industries rely on high quality control standards to export products, mostly to home plants in the United States.

Due to the strong desire of the elites for imported goods, Haiti has historically operated one of the lowest and most open tariffs in the world. This is changing under pressure from local entrepreneurs who, in 1982, convinced the government to ban imports of coffee, candies, soap, shoes, vinegar, bread, matches, and other items for two years in order to encourage import substitution with locally produced items.

While the external donors insist that agriculture should be the priority, the Haitian government has put its limited funds into a new sugar mill, L'Usine Sucrière de Léogane, the fourth in the country, a vegetable oil mill, SODEXOL, and an international fishing fleet. These projects create very few new jobs at enormous capital cost, and they will require substan-

TABLE 4.2:
Industrial Enterprises at Port-au-Prince

	Number of Enterprises	Employment
Clothing[a]	54	10,109
Electronic Components[b]	25	6,259
Baseballs	12	4,636
Beverages[c]	12	784
Textiles	12	1,107
Food Products	11	1,405
Furniture	10	911
Leather Products	10	1,182
Toys	9	1,092
Footwear	7	1,594
Metal Products	7	852
Paper and Printing	5	136
Chemical Products[d]	4	911
Essential Oils	3	629
Building Materials	2	144
Cement	1	360
Steel Products	1	157
Miscellaneous	16	1,622
Total	201	33,890

[a]Including embroidery
[b]Including tapes
[c]Including alcohol distilleries
[d]Paints, industrial gases, soap, detergents

Source: Ministry of Planning. List of industrial enterprises at Port-au-Prince metropolitan area. June 30, 1979.

tial subsidies and protection.[30] One observer estimated that the fishing fleet provided 166 new jobs at an investment of $142,700 per worker.

Several careful studies have indicated about $26 million a year in annual imports to Haiti that could be replaced by import-substitution industries.[31] These would be mostly small-scale enterprises in pharmaceuticals, chemicals, metals, and a few other fields. They might need some initial start-up protection, but they could prove profitable. They do not, however, offer ample suppliers' credits or opportunities for kickbacks if they are to be monitored by external donors who would provide some of the funding. Hence, the government's preference for its own unmonitored deals. Whatever the outcome, industrial import substitution at best can create several thousand new jobs, save some foreign exchange, and provide industrial training. It is not a substitute for positive action about agriculture.

BASEBALLS

Export assembly industries are a global phenomenon to be found in Puerto Rico, Singapore, Taiwan, Hong Kong, Mexico, Haiti, and elsewhere. Their operating principle is to take advantage of lower labor costs by locating the labor-intensive part of a manufacturing process wherever those costs are lowest. Suitable infrastructure, quality control, reliable and reasonably priced transportation, level of local taxes, and other factors are also important. Export industries were first introduced into Puerto Rico in the 1940s and by the 1960s a few had moved to Haiti as Puerto Rican labor costs rapidly increased. The Haitian government moved quickly to provide tax incentives (5 year exemption and then reduced payment for another five years), duty free imports of components, an industrial estate in the capital, the promise of an adequate electrical supply, and most importantly a guaranteed able, inexpensive, and docile labor force (mostly unskilled urban women). A further advantage was the enactment in 1962 of U.S. Customs Code Sections 806 and 807 "which permit goods assembled from U.S.-made components to reenter the U.S. with duty paid only on the value added abroad."[32] The U.S. Department of Commerce advertises that under the 806 and 807 provisions American companies can establish themselves in Haiti with a minimal capital investment and can profit from the lower minimum wage of $.033 per hour or $2.64 per day, which is what most of the 45,000 to 50,000 workers in these industries earn, although they are paid by the piece. It is generally understood that the government will repress strikes and interdict independent trade unions.

The steady influx of new labor into the capital, where the industries are located, also helps maintain an obedient labor force fearful of losing jobs. The industries are not, however, a direct cause of migration to Port-au-Prince. Grunwald, Delatour, and Voltaire found that "workers had been in Port-au-Prince an average of 14 years, long before the assembly industries emerged as a significant force in Haiti's economic development.[33]

Haiti has become a reliable and efficient exporter of baseballs, clothing, electronics, souvenirs to be sold at such unlikely places as U.S. Indian reservations, and other items. A baseball sewn by hand in Haiti is assessed by U.S. Customs only on the value of the labor added. The republic has thus become the largest producer of finished baseballs in the world.

It is clear who is benefiting from these industries, whose exports to the United States increased from $9.1 million in 1971 to $153.8 million in 1980. First, the owners who earn 15 to 20 percent a year tax-free on their investments. Considering that similar factories in Mexico pay higher minimum wages plus social security or almost twice the rate in Haiti, the advantages to firms in Port-au-Prince are clear. The Haitian government is also benefiting through indirect and direct taxes on the workers and from construction by the firms. Third, the workers, two-thirds of whom are women, gain from the chance to work and to earn, from formal and informal on-the-job training and from some limited medical services. But their wages are too low partly because the employers keep them low and put pressure on the government not to raise the minimum. Fourth, several hundred Haitian entrepreneurs and technicians own or manage export plants and constitute a new social group.

Owners united in the Association of Haitian Industries (ADIH) have complained there is no "realistic" wage policy in the country. They say that at the present rate of increase the daily wage will reach $4.50 in 1983 which, in their view, will make Haitian products much less competitive. And they protest the 19 legal holidays, a wage of time and one-half (or a 50 percent premium) on overtime compared with 25 percent in Brazil and 30 percent in the Dominican Republic. Night shift workers are supposed to be paid at a rate one and one-half times day workers, thus discouraging owners and managers from recruiting night shifts. It is difficult to know how seriously one should take these complaints as some workers claim the owners do not observe the above laws anyway.

The business community has also complained, with more justification, that there are too many levies on their workers. The average worker in a baseball plant must contribute $74.66 or 9.06 percent of his or her annual wages of about $823.68 to the government in nine different taxes including one ironically called "Contribution for Economic Liberation." These taxes reduce purchasing power, discourage the worker, and put pressure on industries to raise wages which they do not wish to do. Entrepreneurs also encourage the government to build low-cost housing for Port-au-Prince workers, improve transportation and the water supply. These are rational suggestions from the point of view of plant managers and owners who wish to maximize profits. Their quest for profit is also a source for reform in Haiti. They complain to the government about corruption, about the macoute-inspired smuggling from the Dominican Republic which undermines Haitian businesses, and about problems of infrastructure. Their reports to the government are naturally self-serving, but an improvement in their own security should help the entire Haitian economy. An example is the tomato paste industry. Local plants employing Haitians purchase tomatoes from Haitian farmers and produce the paste for a local market estimated at over $40 million a year. Recently tonton macoute leaders and Arab traders have been bringing in foreign-produced paste without paying the requisite customs. They have been able to undersell the local industry, and two companies have closed because of this corruption.[34] Although employers may express their views, which they could not have done under François Duvalier, workers are not free to organize or to speak out.

Haitian entrepreneurs hold their own. According to one study "almost 40 percent of the firms in the sample are Haitian-owned, one-third are foreign owned, and 30 percent are joint ventures."[35] Haitian-owned and joint venture operations sign contracts with American firms to supply finished clothing or other items, the parts of which are shipped to Haiti. Often machinery is lent to the firms by American corporations which facilitates Haitian entrepreneurs entering the industry.

Some assembly plants are also beginning to establish links to local industries. For instance cassette assembly plants purchase plastic shells from a local producer; the cores of baseballs and softballs are now fabricated in Haiti and the glue is supplied locally.[36] Local leather is used for glove making operations.

The principal value of these plants remains the annual wages they pay of $30–40 million. The number of people—family members as well as workers themselves—dependent on industrial workers' salaries has been estimated at between 260,000 and 325,000, or about one-third of the Port-au-Prince population. This figure is still much smaller than the number of people dependent on coffee, but it is likely to increase.

Business people and industrialists are urging the government to pass new laws facilitating industrial expansion, cutting down on corruption and bureaucratic red tape, and protecting local markets. They complain that despite past expansion, Haiti only accounted for 1.2 percent of the U.S. imports of products under the 806 and 807 provisions compared with 17.9 percent for Mexico.[37] Enactment of the tariff-free provisions of the U.S. Caribbean Basin Initiative would also help Haiti, but these have run into some U.S. business and labor opposition.

Industrialists further complain that their total payroll charges equal 37.43 percent of production costs compared with 28.92 percent in the Dominican Republic and 19.08 percent in Indonesia. It is not clear how the government will react to these complaints, but what is interesting is the dynamism and collective calculation of self-interest among plant owners and managers. Complain as they might about taxation, the industries themselves are tax exempt and owners, like other middle-class Haitians, pay little income tax. Their net contribution to the Haitian economy consists of their local wages and salaries and transfer of technology. They offer hope, but they are no substitute for agriculture.

MINING AND AGRICULTURAL PROCESSING

Mining and agricultural transformation industries have a troubled history in Haiti. Because they are dependent on large-scale foreign investment and technology and the possible alienation of land, they touch sensitive Haitian nerves. The HAMPCO meat-packing plant exports to Puerto Rico and elsewhere its refrigerated meat, but does not raise cattle to rebuild the herd. The sisal decorticating factory remains from a 1940s effort to establish sisal plantations in the northeast, much to the opposition of local farmers. Now it depends on those same farmers, pays low prices, and operates an antiquated plant. The four sugar mills have Haitian government and local capital and pay erratic prices to poorly motivated local farmers. The amount of sugar extracted from the cane is also much lower than in neighboring countries.

Most controversial of all has been the Reynolds Company concession to extract bauxite. It is a classic enclave operation as the U.S. company built its own roads, a port at Miragoane, a company town, and schools. After obtaining the right to mine from the Magloire administration the company expanded their operations in the early years of Dr. Duvalier's presidency and consistently paid the Haitians less for their bauxite than they paid to Jamaicans. Haiti was able to renegotiate higher royalties after 1974 following the examples of Jamaica and the International Bauxite Association.[38]

The capital-intensive operation never employed more than 400 Haitians, many skilled or semiskilled. There was minimal vertical integration with the Haitian economy and the principal benefits have been in the forms of royalties and taxes, the brunt of the controversy. Reynolds first produced about 500,000 tons and later 400,000 tons of bauxite a year for refining and transformation in North America into aluminun. In the 1970s its bauxite exports averaged $18 to $20 million a year of which the Haitian government received $5 to $6 million.

It has been charged that Dr. Duvalier failed to represent Haitian interests effectively with Reynolds, that his government lacked technical competence or advice, that it sought too low a percentage of royalties, and that it failed to consult with other bauxite producers such as Jamaica and Guyana in the 1950s and 1960s.[39] There is considerable validity in these charges although the government of Jean-Claude Duvalier did receive a higher return. It should also be remembered that Haiti was negotiating low-grade deposits for which there were few interested parties. Since the closing of the mine in 1983, Reynolds-Haiti belongs to history, and Haiti has no other known commercial mineral prospects.

The most impressive economic success story comes from Haitian crafts where individual producers benefit. Crafts exports have increased from $2.3 million in 1965 to $19 million in 1979. Exports to the United States include works of art, wood furniture, brooms, brushes, buttons, carpets, rugs, mats, and textiles, often produced in projects sponsored by CARE and other donors.

Haitian crafts have also found markets through the Caribbean, sometimes disguised as local ware. For instance, a painter in the poor Carrefour area near Port-au-Prince regularly receives wood spoons from a merchant on Nassau in the Bahamas. He paints a map of Nassau Island on the spoon for a few cents. The spoons are collected by the merchant and sold as souveniers in the Bahamas. Similar examples can be cited throughout the Caribbean and as far away as Cayenne, French Guyana, where a chic gallery specializes in Haitian paintings.

TOURISM

Tourism is often considered to be Haiti's most promising economic sector. But its performance has never come close to its promise, and its problems are difficult to resolve. Haitian tourism is highly seasonal, November to April, and, as elsewhere in the Caribbean, for the other months there is excess capacity and underemployment. Visitors, primarily from Canada and the United States, have been numbering 300,000 a year, but about 60 percent arrive on cruise ships and spend only a few hours in the capital or Cap Haïtien.[40] Others purchase package tours from European operators of Club Med or American agents. Thus, tourist expenditures in Haiti are very low compared to the number of visitors which, in any case, amounts to about one-third of the tourists visiting Jamaica or the Dominican Republic.

There are also problems with Haitian tourist attractions. Little has been done to develop their potential, another sign of government indifference. There are few attractive and advertised beaches. Yet numerous small, natural beaches dot the shore. Unlike the Dominican Republic they are not being developed. Henri Christophe's ruined palace, Sans Souci, and his spectacular fortress, La Ferrière, are not easily accessible. Other fortresses and interesting sites of important events in Haitian history are abandoned. Modest but excellent museums operate on contributions and minuscule budgets, while tour operators steer visitors to garish galleries.

The Haitian image is also a problem. Reports of planned or attempted coups, violations of human rights, and political instability have a chilling effect on foreigners seeking the Caribbean sun. The money spent by the Ministry of Tourism on public relations campaigns has done little to alter these images.

INFRASTRUCTURE

Haiti's transport infrastructure is singularly deficient. The Port Authority has developed Port-au-Prince at the expense of all other ports and it now handles 90 percent of external trade.

The railroads came late to Haiti and have been plagued with financial scandals and operating problems. A scant sixty miles of line remains in use north from the capital to a sugar mill. If railroads came late, commercial aviation scarcely came at all. A lilliputian government domestic airline, Air Haiti, shares the one or two serviceable planes of the Air Force for irregular internal flights. Otherwise all international air freight and passenger travel is via foreign carriers who largely hold Haiti at their mercy.

Road transport by contrast is decentralized and mostly in individual hands. There are few large trucking or passenger bus firms and thousands of owners or part-owners of one to four colorful, ancient, and crowded vehicles known as "tap taps" ply the roads. The tap taps are the heart of the labor-intensive, low-cost marketing system, and any increase in the cost of gasoline or diesel fuel is reflected quickly in their costs and prices. Slowly the paved road network is being extended and with U.S. AID funding the job of road maintenance is being tackled. Yet poor roads or lack of any roads continue to isolate the majority of the population, and lack of maintenance often threatens to erode the roads that are paved.

EXTERNAL TRADE

By 1981, ten years after Dr. Duvalier's death, exports increased five-fold to $226 million annually, but imports increased more than seven-fold to $411,700,000 producing a giant deficit of almost $200 million. Earnings from tourism, foreign aid, private investment, remittances, and external borrowing, the traditional ways of offsetting visible trade deficits, have not been able to cover this imbalance. Prior to a 1982 International Monetary Fund loan of over $30 million, Haiti's external debt had climbed to $277.3 million with interest payments annually of $17.8 million.

Haiti's growing trade deficits reflect low-world coffee prices, decline in coffee exports, rising costs of fuel (a gallon of gasoline sold for $2.15 in 1982), and consistent import demands for processed foods, vehicles, and manufactured goods. Consumer goods account for two-thirds of imports with investment goods absorbing only one-third, a negative sign for future development prospects.

PUBLIC SECTOR

The public sector in Haiti generally works badly and sometimes not at all. The central government accounts for about 10 percent of GDP and the public utilities and other parastatals for another 10 percent. The role of the public sector in the economy is therefore much less than it is in North America or Western Europe. Haiti is predominantly an open, private enterprise economy. The public sector serves particularly as an instrument of redistribution from poor to rich.

The major public utilities (electricity, water, telecommunications, port, and flour mill) have generally been off the government budget. All have earned profits in recent years except for water. All provide inferior services almost exclusively to the urban areas. Some of the profits have been used to finance foreign loans for capital equipment. Other off-budget revenues have included taxes on essential oils, taxes on Haitians recruited to cut sugar cane in the Dominican Republic, and commissions charged by the Régie du Tabac on cement, flour, sugar, vegetable oil, cigarettes, and matches. Since Haitians wishing to travel must pay $30 for an exit visa, consular fees are a windfall. Another off-budget item is the National Lottery, which takes in $500,000 a year. The government has also raised the airport departure tax for all travelers from $4.00 to $10.00.

MONEY

One of the saving graces of this disorderly administration has been an orderly monetary system since the occupation. The Haitian gourde has been fully convertible and tied to the U.S. dollar, which also circulates as legal tender. Past memories of nineteenth-century currency debasement, and the equivalency of the dollar and the gourde kept the money sound and the economy open. Until about 1982 the currency black market was unknown. The National Bank cautiously regulates the amount of dollars and gourdes in circulation. There is no stock exchange, bond, or treasury note market and little way internally to mobilize savings. The National Bank established a separate commercial bank in 1978 to fill part of the void in Haitian private banking.

Fuel costs, combined with government deficits, have brought inflation close to 20 percent annual levels in recent years. Monetary policy itself though is mostly passive and follows International Monetary Fund advice, and until the 1980s foreswore massive external borrowings. The National Bank is one of the few Haitian institutions that can be said to be institutionalized. Its strength is the national fear that another round of currency debasement and unpaid overseas loans could again jeopardize Haitian sovereignty. Thus there is an elite consensus on the need for a conservative monetary policy and for giving the National Bank enough autonomy to carry it out. However, large-scale corruption, trade deficits, smuggling, and mismanagement, which have limited the availability of dollars, have given rise to a small black market in U.S. currency since about 1982. The same factors have forced the government to borrow from the International Monetary Fund. A weakened economy, which these trends indicate, poses a political risk for the regime because the exporters, middlemen, and middlewomen will withdraw their support from Jean-Claude Duvalier if their livelihood is threatened.

CONCLUSION: HAITIAN POLITICAL ECONOMY

The Haitian economy is directly responsible for much of the instability and violence in Haitian politics throughout its history. There are few secure sources of wealth and income in Haiti. Access to wealth and income depends on control of the government and taxes. Hence the intensity and persistence of intra-elite factions and their constant struggle for power.

Politics is a zero-sum game in which winners—those who control the government and their allies—have access to considerable wealth in a desperately poor society. The losers—those who no longer control the government or have been deprived of allies in the government—have no access to significant wealth. If one does not adhere to a faction, one can be victimized by all sides in Haiti's first world. As a result, factions have been far more important than political institutions such as parties or trade unions. Universalistic ideologies or belief systems, longterm programs for political or economic development, and even educational resources are irrelevant. This is pirate politics on a rudderless ship.

NOTES

1. Mats Lundahl, "The Roots of Haitian Underdevelopment" (Paper prepared for symposium, "Haiti: Present State and Future Prospects," Wingspread Foundation, Racine, Wisconsin, 23–26 September 1982.)

2. Calculations derived from "Budget Général de l'Exercice 1981-82," *Le Moniteur: Journal Officiel de le République d'Haïti*, 28 September 1981, pp. 50–57.

3. Grégoire Eugène, "Mémoire à l'OEA", in *Haïti-Observateur* (26 November–December 1982), p. 7.

4. Current Haitian Government Revenues, 1975–79, International Monetary Fund, Banque Nationale.

5. "Budget Général de l'Exercice 1981–1982, October 1981–September 1982", p. 107.

6. Georges Anglade, *L'Espace haïtien* (Montreal: Editions des Alizés, 1981), pp. 88–111.

7. Christian A. Girault, *Le commerce du café en Haïti: Habitants, spéculateurs, et exportateurs* (Mémoire de Centre d' Etudes de Géographie Tropicale-Bordeaux (Paris: CNRS, 1981), p. 95.

8. Georges Anglade, *Espace et liberte en Haïti* (Montreal: ERCE and CRC, 1982), p. 20.

9. Robert Maguire, remarks at symposium, "Haiti: Present State and Future Prospects," (Wingspread Foundation, Racine, Wisconsin, 23–26 September 1982). Maguire specializes on Haiti at the Inter American Development Foundation.

10. F. Morisseau-Leroy, *Récolte* (Port-au-Prince: Les Editions Haïtiennes, 1946).

11. Lundahl, "Roots of Haitian Underdevelopment," p. 12.

12. Anglade, *L'Espace haïtien*, pp. 17–8. And, Maurice de Young, *Man and Land in the Haitian Economy*, (Gainesville: University of Florida Press, 1958), pp. 47–49.

13. Anglade, *L'Espace haïtien*, pp. 107–8.

14. Ibid., pp. 119–23. Ivan Beghin, William Fougère, Kendall W. King, *L'aliénation et la nutrition en Haïti*, (Paris: Presses Universitaries de France, 1970), pp. 67–110.

15. Gerald F. Murray, "Cash-Cropping Agroforestry: An Anthropological Approach to Agricultural Development in Rural Haiti" (Paper prepared for symposium, "Haiti: Present State and Future Prospects," Wingspread Foundation, Racine, Wisconsin, 23–26 September 1982).

16. Paul Moral, *Le paysan haïtien (Etude sur la vie rurale en Haïti)*, (1961; reprint ed., Port-au-Prince: Fardin 1978), pp. 189–208.

17. Girault, *Le commerce du cafe*, p. 92. We depend here on this recent comprehensive study.

18. Ibid., pp. 71–76.

19. Ibid., p. 92.

20. Ibid., p. 155, citing Gérard Pierre-Charles, an exile Haitian economist teaching in Mexico.

21. Lundhal, "Roots of Haitian Underdevelopment," p. 16.

22. Giovanni Caprio, *Haiti: Wirtschaftliche Entwicklung und periphere Gesell-schaftsformation* (Frankfurt/Main: Haag and Herchen, 1979). Like Caprio, Philippe Rouzier works to build a theory of development and world trade using the example of Haiti. See his *Exchange et développement (Cadre théorique pour une alternative)* (Ottawa: Université d'Ottawa, 1981).

23. Girault, *Le commerce du cafe*, p., 164.

24. Lundahl, "Roots of Haitian Underdevelopment." p. 17.

25. Girault, *Le commerce du cafe*, p. 204.

26. JWK International Corporation, "Coffee Policy Study: Haiti" (Draft, commissioned by US A.I.D., 15 April 1976, p. V-16. Data for this study was for the mid-1970s.

27. Girault, *Le commerce du cafe*, p. 192-93.

28. Ibid., p. 203.

29. Ibid., p. 228.

30. US AID/Haiti, *Country Development Strategy FY 1983-1987*, mimeo-graphed (Port-au-Prince: AID, Jan. 1981), p. 19.

31. International Labor Organization, *Report on Small Enterprises in Haiti*, (Geneva: ILO, 1979).

32. U.S. Department of Commerce interviews, Washington, D.C.

33. Joseph Grunwald, Leslie Delatour, Karl Voltaire, "Offshore Assembly in Haiti," *The Internationalization of Industry* (Washington: Brookings, to be published in 1983), p. 223.

34. Interview with Jean Dominique, 31 May 1983.

35. Grunwald, p. 214-15, manuscript.

36. Ibid.

37. Association des Industries d' Haiti, "The Industrial Sector in Haiti: Situation, Prospects, and Politics," (Port-au-Prince: ADIH, 1981).

38. Monique P. Garrity, "The Multinational Corporation in Extractive Industries: A Case Study of Reynolds Haitian Mines, Inc.," in *Working Papers in Haitian Society and Culture*, ed. Sidney W. Minty (New Haven: Yale University Antilles Research Program, 1975), pp. 209-15.

39. Ibid.

40. *Bulletin Trimestriel de Statistique*, No. 116, 4 éme Trimestre 1979, (Port-au-Prince: IHS, 1979), pp. 41-42.

5

HAITI AND THE WORLD

Haiti was born as a black, officially French-speaking republic. From the beginning this dual racial and linguistic identity has affected its relationship with other countries even though not every citizen was physically black, and only a minority spoke French. It has been a factor in its relative isolation and its pattern of contacts with Africa, France, the Caribbean, and Afro-Americans.

Since 1804, no slave-owning or colonial state could be complacent about this example of blacks in power. After 1915 some Afro-American leaders viewed with concern the American military occupation of Haiti. Recently the French and Canadians have helped the republic in part in the name of language solidarity. In the last decade the plight of poor Haitians emigrating across the Caribbean has been discussed on the first pages of the world's newspapers. In short, the black republic, its leaders, its original culture, contributions and problems have terrified, embarrassed, or fascinated, and summoned up sentiments of race and language solidarity or of pity in other lands. Indifference is impossible for those who know something about Haiti's history and culture.

RACE AND LANGUAGE CONSCIOUSNESS

As early as 1806 Haiti was a focus for the clashing interests between New England traders importing molasses, coffee, sugar, and cotton and

Southern plantation owners. Under pressure from the French to isolate the new black republic, the Southerners led the U.S. Congress to pass a law prohibiting U.S. trade with Haiti. The debate revealed the symbolic importance of Dessalines and his successors. Representatives of slaveholders obviously feared black revolution in their states. On the floor of the U.S. House of Representatives, John Randolph denounced Haiti as "an anomaly among the nations of the earth." In his view, Southerners should "leave nothing undone which could possibly give to the white population in that island an ascendancy over the blacks...."[1] Northern newspapers and traders criticized these measures and attitudes including the refusal to recognize Haiti. Abolitionists fighting for the freedom of blacks understood the international dimension of the struggle and agitated for recognition and diplomatic relations between the United States and Haiti, the two oldest republics in the hemisphere. Even the French, seeking debt repayments and commercial advantages, recognized their former colony in 1825, but the United States waited until Southern voices were muted by the Civil War. In 1862 President Lincoln recognized both Haiti and Liberia.

Antiblack sentiment took new forms in the U.S. and elsewhere as it began to infect the twentieth century. The first two decades marked the institutionalization of segregation in the United States, and a copious racist literature bound to affect white attitudes toward blacks appeared. In this context the white marines occupied Haiti. It is not surprising that military officials and State Department personnel dealing with Haiti shared the negative and biased attitudes then prevalent. Admiral Knapp, an administrator in Haiti, wrote in 1921: "The same traits of Negro character that are found in the United States exist in Haiti, both good and bad; but I consider that the bad traits are more in evidence in Haiti than in the United States, where they are under better control."[2]

Educated Afro-Americans had a different view even though it was distorted by tales about Voodoo, the black and brown struggle for supremacy, and the language barrier; their own battle for equality at home limited their interest in overseas matters. Nonetheless, the abolitionist leader, Frederick Douglass, appointed by President Harrison in 1889 to be U.S. Minister-Resident and Consul-General to Haiti, defended black rule: "It was her one brave example that first of all started the Christian world into a sense of the Negro's manhood."[3] Other Afro-American leaders to the present have displayed a special concern toward the island republic. The NAACP protested the U.S. invasion of Haiti in 1915: "Let us save Hayti," wrote the editorialist of the organization's *The Crisis* magazine in 1915. "Hayti is a noble nation.... It is a nation that made slaves free."[4] Later the NAACP sent its secretary James Weldon Johnson to investigate the U.S.

occupation, and he wrote up his critical findings for *The Nation* magazine. Afro-American scholars such as Rayford Logan, Alain Leroy Locke, and Mercer Cook at Howard University visited Haiti and published informative works. Logan in particular produced important scholarly books including his *The Diplomatic Relations of the United States with Haiti, 1776–1891,* published in 1941. Haitian writers and professors such as Dantès Bellegarde and Maurice Lubin came to the United States and taught at Howard University.

In the 1980s the Congressional Black Caucus in the U.S. House of Representatives has developed an interest in Haiti after the unfair treatment of black Haitian refugees was exposed. They have pressed the government on immigration matters, for additional aid funds, and have urged the Haitian government to respect human rights. Two black members of Congress, Walter Fauntroy and Shirley Chisolm, traveled to Port-au-Prince as part of the Caucus Task Force on Haitian Refugees in 1982; they publicly assured Haitians of their solidarity: "Black Americans and Haitians are part of an involuntary African diaspora. The only difference between us is that the slave ships stopped at different points in the Americas. We are cousins in the African family and it is in this spirit that we come on our fact-finding mission to Haiti seeking to tell the truth in love, to face reality with courage, and to work effectively as legislators in the United States House of Representatives."[5] Congressman Fauntroy returned in December 1982 accompanied by staff including Stephen Horblitt who has a longterm interest in Haiti. Horblitt also observed municipal elections in 1983, and the Congressman protested the arrest of some prominent Haitians during those elections.

Despite some embarrassment about the first black republic, French-speaking African intellectuals have felt kinship with Haitians, too. In particular, they knew and appreciated Haitian literature. Léopold Sédar Senghor, noted poet and then President of Senegal, visited the country, symbolizing his respect for the Haitian contribution to black and world culture.

The Haitian elites viewed their country as a beacon of freedom for the colonized of the world and as a black republic carrying the traditions of France into the New World. Thus, they supported the Greek independence movement.[6] They supported Simón Bolivar who took refuge in Haiti, and they expressed their enthusiasm in 1898 for the freedom movement in Cuba while expressing their fears of U.S. intervention which might abort it. Dantès Bellegarde and Auguste Nemours denounced white South Africa and Fascist Italy in the League of Nations.[7]

Intellectuals and educators followed the affairs of blacks in the United

States of America. President Boyer opened the gates to any blacks, free or enslaved, who wished to come to Haiti. Jean Price-Mars, who visited Tuskegee Institute, believed that his compatriots could learn from the educational experience of Booker T. Washington as well as provide hope for Afro-Americans. Hannibal Price, a Haitian diplomat and historian articulated best the racial role of Haiti in the white dominated world: Haitians, in his view, were the only blacks in the nineteenth and early twentieth centuries who could think and act like free men and women. In control of their own destiny, Haitians would build a free nation meriting the respect of others. By freely charting their destiny and showing the skeptical world what blacks could accomplish on their own, Haiti would "rehabilitate the black race."[8] Therefore, Price continued, Haiti's struggle "is important for the whole black race:" social prejudice will end with "the moral victory of the Republic of Haiti against ill will and against the international antipathy which still exists almost everywhere."[9] Poets and essayists put the same message in a different language. Moved by the shocking lynchings in the American South, poet Jean F. Brierre composed the following:

> When you bleed, Harlem, my handkerchief turns crimson.
> When you weep, your lament is prolonged in my song.
> With the same fervor, and through the same dark night,
> Black brother, both of us dream the same dream.[10]

The school boys in Morisseau-Leroy's novel *Récolte* "felt solidarity with the youth of Europe and Asia, Africa and Latin America. They knew by heart the verses of Langston Hughes translated by René Piquion."[11]

Identification with France took precedence over racial consciousness for most of the elite before 1915, but Price-Mars explained that Haitians could be proud of both their French and African heritages which they have woven together over the years in an original way. In a speech at the Sorbonne he declared that his country successfully combined the "intuition, feeling and affection of the Negro with the clarity, measure and order of the French mind in order to fashion the Haitian soul."[12] Haitian poet René Depestre notes the importance attached to the 1945 visit to Haiti of the white and black French intellectuals, André Breton and Aimé Césaire. Surrealism, existentialism, socialism, and other French currents of thought inspired Depestre and his friends, who published a special issue of their literary review, *La Ruche*, in honor of Breton. They said they found in surrealism, about which he lectured, a justification for rebellion against fascism in the world at large and against the emptiness of politics at home.[13]

In short, Haitians could weep for a John Brown, a Haile Selassie, and a Dr. Martin Luther King, Jr. while honoring and sensing a bond with French leaders and intellectuals as well.

Contemporary educated Haitians follow with fascination the victories and defeats of blacks and French-speaking people everywhere. They particularly take pride in the rise of J.F. Peña Gomez, a black man of Haitian origins, who is now mayor of Santo Domingo and secretary general of the ruling Dominican Revolutionary Party or PRD. Haitians identify with the Dominican politician who asserts his Haitian origins in a country where anti-Haitian prejudice is strong. Educated Haitians also sympathize with efforts in Quebec for culture and language promotion.

Race and language have also proved to be an intellectual trap. Believing that blacks are innately different from whites drew Jean Price-Mars and François Duvalier dangerously close to the ideas of Gobineau, an intellectual source for racism in Europe, and to world fascism of the 1930s and 1940s. As late as 1944, for example, Duvalier made a passing but approving reference to the rhetoric of Alfred Rosenberg, the most radical Nazi ideologue.[14] Obsession with race, like the obsession with the Haitian revolution, obscures analysis of real problems facing Haiti today. Price-Mars understood this and near the end of his life felt the need to warn his compartiots that race consciousness should not deflect attention from other forms of social division such as class, an important basis for exploitation.[15]

ISOLATION

Isolation from the rest of the world is a major theme in Haitian self-perceptions despite their intense race solidarity. One journalist complained in 1982: "We have the appearance of an isolated, misunderstood and ignored country in the Caribbean itself. We don't belong to the British Commonwealth; we don't have access to the Caribbean Common Market (Caricom), and they never admitted us to the Lomé Convention."[16] (The Lomé Convention is the trade and aid agreement between the European Community and a large group of developing countries.) Haiti has been isolated diplomatically during much of its history. For example, from independence to the 1860s Haiti had no formal relations with the United States or the Vatican. Dr. Duvalier's regime was marked by very limited contacts between Haiti and the outside world. In 1983 only 20 countries maintain ambassadors resident in Port-au-Prince.

Throughout the nineteenth and during much of the twentieth century

Haiti was the only or one of the few independent states in the Caribbean. Britain and France sought to minimize its contacts with their dependencies. Thus the attainment of independence by a dozen English-speaking Caribbean countries since 1960 found them knowing little about their neighbor and vice-versa. Haiti has been on the periphery of the Caribbean blocs which have emerged at the UN and in the Organization of American States, separated culturally and linguistically and by its political regime from its Commonwealth Caribbean neighbors.

Although Haiti supported their independence from Spain, the white, mulatto, and mestizo rulers of these new Latin American countries emphasized the linguistic and racial differences between themselves and the followers of Dessalines, Christophe, and Pétion. Haiti was grudgingly admitted into the Pan-American Union which later became the OAS, with French sparingly recognized as one of the official languages. Ties with Latin America have tended to be formal, distant, and aloof, marked by little interest on either side.

DOMINICAN REPUBLIC

Haiti's relations with its island sharer have a character all of their own. The twenty-year Haitian occupation is still resented, and many Dominicans credit their independence in 1844 to their struggle against oppressive Haitian rule, rather than against three centuries of oppressive Spanish rule. On the Haitian side, memories of the 1937 massacre have not dimmed, even though it is ignored in official histories. In their diplomatic relations with the U.S. during the nineteenth century and at other times, Dominicans have emphasized their relative "whiteness" against the threat of black Haitians coming into their territory.

Haitian migration began during the colonial period, when runaway slaves from Haiti found refuge in Santo Domingo where the Spanish authorities allowed them to settle rather than returning them to the French. During the period of Haitian domination of Santo Domingo, there was extensive "Haitianization" of the border areas. The border itself was not finally demarcated until 1935. The Dominican sugar boom which began in the 1880s used Haitian labor from the outset, despite the antagonism toward blacks which led to the massacre in 1937.

Yet Dominican-Haitian relations are more than rancor, conflict, and isolation. Political leaders have often cultivated business and personal ties, and each capital has served at times as a sanctuary for groups in exile. Since the death of Trujillo in 1962 the temporary migration of Haitian cane-cutters has been resumed and become an important source of government to government contact. From 1966 to 1971 a government to government agreement existed which was not renewed, but both governments continue to act as if it exists. The Haitian government receives a payment for each Haitian migrant recruited to work in the Dominican Republic. The Dominicans use the Haitians on state and privately owned sugar estates and benefit from low wages and poor working conditions which keep sugar export costs down. The arrangements have proved lucrative for both governments. Lacking opportunities to earn cash in Haiti, the voluntarily recruited workers have no organizations and little protection. A 1983 report to the International Labor Office concluded workers are not paid what they are due, their housing is inadequate, their hours on the job are excessive, the Haitian government makes a profit from recruitment. In short, the "Government of Haiti... has been associated with the measures which contravene the Abolition of Forced Labour Convention and has derived benefit from them."[17] At present there are an estimated 200,000 Haitians in the Dominican Republic including sugar and coffee workers, rural squatters and city dwellers.[18]

The heart of Dominican-Haitian relations is whether one or both sides seeks to destabilize politically or overthrow the other. During his 30-year rule Trujillo was assured of having Haitian governments that were no threat. Dr. Duvalier even allowed Dominican forces to patrol the Haitian coast to prevent feared Cuban landings. Since the onset of democratically elected governments in the Dominican Republic in 1968 and the peaceful transfers of civilian power, Dominican involvement in Haitian politics has visibly diminished. Haitian exiles no longer find ready acceptance in Santo Domingo, and the two governments have held a series of meetings to study border projects and other matters. Nor has the Haitian government, covertly or overtly, sought to influence rapidly evolving Dominican politics. Franklin Franco, who has long sought ways of improving relations between the two countries, became Dominican Minister of Education in 1982. Soon thereafter he instructed school book publishers to alter the image of Haiti in student's textbooks.[19]

The easing of political tensions brought about a sharp rise in legal and contraband intraisland trade. "From 1971 to 1980 Dominican exports to Haiti went from $100,000 to $10,000,000."[20] Although intraisland trade is much less than 5 percent of the total trade of either country, its growth reflects the improvement in roads, telecommunications, banking, tourism, and other contacts. Others who have benefited include soldiers on both sides of the border, tontons macoutes, coffee exporters, and other participants in the lively contraband trade.

Racial feelings, powerful historical emotions, and other sharp differences remain. The Dominican Republic and Haiti have just begun to learn to live together peacefully on the same island.

FOREIGN ECONOMIC INFLUENCE

Haiti has probably been the least economically dependent state in the Caribbean.[21] Its total foreign private investment is half that of the Dominican Republic; a third that of Jamaica. Its dependence on the U.S. for half its imports and exports is less than that of most of its neighbors, including Cuba with two-thirds of its trade with the Soviet Union. Very little Haitian land has been permanently alienated to foreign interests. Although persons of Lebanese and Syrian origin have an extensive role in foreign trade, their origins in Haiti go back to the turn of the century, and many have acquired Haitian nationality and families.

Economic nationalism has not protected Haiti from outside economic influence. Haitian history is marked by laws against foreign land ownership and participation in trade, but they have been mostly honored in the breach. Instead Haiti's deep poverty and lack of resources has served to curb foreign economic appetites. President Jean-Claude Duvalier has gone further than most Haitian leaders in soliciting foreign involvement but, with the exception of the export assembly industries, the response has been limited. The decline in the economy may make him more dependent on foreign assistance than any of his predecessors, however.

France

French economic influence in Haiti has been long surpassed by cultural influence. France buys some coffee, sells some machinery, but generally is a minor trading partner. The monopoly cement company is French-owned but there has been no new major French private investment for many years. French official aid lags behind that of Canada and West Germany.

The most significant French influence is clearly cultural. The Institut Français d'Haïti is a leading cultural center, and has provided in the past a major forum for Haitian intellectuals such as Price-Mars. A French firm won the contract to install the color TV system which relies on imported French and U.S. programs. French influence is still marked in the elite secondary schools, the older faculty at the University of Haiti, and in Catholic church circles. Haiti also takes part in worldwide franchophone organizations in which the French government plays a leading role.

Canada

Canadian involvement in Haiti has grown significantly in recent years. Canadian exports to Haiti increased from $15.9 million (Canadian) in 1977 to $30.0 million in 1979, while Haitian exports to Canada increased from $3.4 million to $6.6 million Canadian during the same period.[22] Canada has become a major donor.

During the last ten years special ties have been forged between Haiti and the Province of Quebec. Most of the 25,000 Haitians resident in Canada live in Quebec. Tourism to Haiti has grown rapidly. Much of the pressure for Canadian aid to Haiti comes from Quebec and much of the aid is administered by French-speaking Canadians. There is a shared sense of being two isolated French-speaking communities in a world dominated by the North American colossus, and a willingness to share experiences.

United States

U.S. influence in Haiti dwarfs that of all others. This influence has grown appreciably over the decade of Jean-Claude Duvalier's presidency mostly due to internal momentum rather than any formal push. The increase in activities by U.S.-based nongovernmental organizations, called Private Voluntary Organizations, has been particularly pronounced. An estimated 112 American PVO's are currently working in Haiti. They may be divided into three broad categories: religious, humanitarian, and developmental. The religious PVO's include the Seventh-Day Adventist World Service, the Albert Schweitzer Memorial Hospital, and a number of Catholic, Baptist, and other groups. Humanitarian PVO's include Foster Parents, Friends of Children, and others. Development-oriented PVO's in Haiti include CARE, Church World Service, and the Pan-American Development Foundation. Distribution of surplus U.S. food under Public Law 480 is primarily handled by CARE, the Seventh-Day Adventists, Catholic Relief Services, and Church World Service.

The U.S. has been Haiti's major trading partner even before the arrival of the marines in 1915. Haiti exports coffee, baseballs, and other products and imports machinery and consumer goods running a deficit on current account as it has for many years. Revenues from tourism, U.S. aid, remittances from Haitians working in the U.S., and loans and new investments partly cover the deficit. According to the Department of Commerce, U.S. private investment stands at about $140 million; more than half of all private investment in Haiti, but minuscule compared to U.S. holdings elsewhere in the Caribbean (e.g., $400 million in Jamaica). One company, Gulf and Western, has a larger investment in the Dominican Republic than the total of all U.S. private investment in Haiti.

Haitians also have invested heavily in the United States although no reliable estimates are available. Some Haitians resident in Haiti have become U.S. citizens, and others have used their investments abroad to guarantee U.S. travel visas for business purposes. The United States has become the sanctuary of preference for Haitians seeking to protect their assets and futures.

Since World War II official U.S. support for trade and investments in Haiti has been intermittent. The Export-Import Bank has provided $40 million in loans to promote U.S. exports but has in recent years pulled back lending in Haiti due to problems of defaults and low credit-worthiness.[23] The Overseas Private Insurance Corporation (OPIC) provides insurance for investors but has done little business in Haiti.

U.S. trade laws have had more impact. The General System of Preferences for developing countries established in 1974 enables almost $30 million a year of Haitian exports to enter the U.S. duty-free. U.S. tariff provisions in favor of offshore assembly industries have been particularly valuable to Haiti. The U.S. Caribbean Basin Initiative allows more Haitian goods to enter duty-free for a 12-year period.

FOREIGN POLITICAL INFLUENCE

Foreign political influence—U.S., French, or any other—is more difficult to measure than economic relationships. Like their small neighbors in the Caribbean, many Haitians inside and outside governing circles share "the perception that the United States shapes all events."[24] A sense of powerlessness and frustration tempts them to blame or to give credit to the U.S. for the survival of the Duvalier regime. Signs of the U.S. presence are easily seen. The U.S. coast guard ship regularly docks at Port-au-Prince after towing into port the boats allegedly making their way illegally to North America. The Coast Guard also is part of a small training program for the Haitian navy. Haitian rulers are sensitive to American official attitudes and gestures. During the Carter administration from 1976 to 1980, U.S. diplomats urged Jean-Claude Duvalier and his ministers to accept the democratic opposition and a human rights movement of very modest proportions. These pressures have lessened under the Reagan administration. More importantly, Haiti, like several other small states, has considerable leverage over U.S. policy makers from both Democratic and Republican parties.

The world threat of communist expansion, Cuban actions, what is seen as the "loss" of Iran, Grenada, and Nicaragua and the proximity of Caribbean islands to the United States influence perceptions of interest. Policy makers in Washington, Ottawa, and Paris claim there are no alternatives to the various noncommunist authoritarian regimes they support. Edwin M. Martin, a former assistant secretary of state for InterAmerican Affairs, has reported that President John F. Kennedy wished to see Dr. Duvalier replaced, but the October 1962 missile crisis convinced State Department specialists that America could not afford to undermine Cuba's anticommunist neighbors lest the Soviet Union profit from any upheavals likely to occur. The State Department informed President Kennedy that the only way to avoid chaos or a communist takeover in Haiti after the disappearance of Dr. Duvalier would be to send in a U.S. occupation force which, coming so soon after the Bay of Pigs disaster, would have been a serious blow to American prestige and interests.[25] Haiti is currently seen as of little political importance in Washington, but the United States provides modest support for the status quo because of a desire for an orderly anticommunist government in Port-au-Prince. As long as the U.S. possesses a base at Guantánamo, Cuba, across the Windward Passage, Haiti's military significance to the U.S. is also minimal. Legally America can keep that base in perpetuity. The Caribbean and Central America are increasingly volatile, and it is difficult to predict Haiti's future importance to military planners. Many Haitians believe the U.S. Navy wishes to set up a base at the Môle St. Nicolas on the Haitian side of the Windward Passage and that ships land there from time to time, but U.S. military and diplomatic authorities deny both assertions.

In our judgment U.S. influence does not keep the Duvalier family in power. Some proof comes from the treatment of Haitian political exiles who have been able to plot and to train in the United States, and to surprise the Haitian government with their attacks. They were neither supported nor effectively discouraged by Washington. Instead, in accordance with U.S. law, those obviously attempting to use American soil as a base for the overthrow of a foreign government with which the United States has diplomatic relations have been arrested. (Title 18 of the U.S. Code, Section 96.) Thus Bernard Sansariq, a Haitian-born gasoline station owner in Florida, was arrested on his way to Haiti by U.S forces in January 1982.

He claimed his goal was the overthrow of Jean-Claude Duvalier. A court sentenced him to three years on probation, a rather mild punishment.[26] Similarly, in March 1982 the FBI arrested a group at sea en route to Haiti, and the Venezuelan police announced the arrest of 15 Haitians in training to overthrow the regime.[27] Joel Deeb, a member of an organization in Florida called the Haitian Coalition of Liberation, was acquitted by a U.S court in June 1983 of the accusation of participating in an attack on Haiti. Both pro- and anti-Duvalier political organizations operate freely in New York and Miami. On the Dominican side, authorities have intercepted a Haitian exile courier and an arms shipment, but other organizations operate peacefully. As far as we know, not even the Cuban government has provided support for a serious exile invasion of Haiti.

Direct U.S. military assistance to the Haitian government amounted to $6 million in loans and grants for the period 1946 to 1980.[28] Add to this a small private arms sale of $1 million, approved by Washington in 1970–71, and the licensed sale of radio-jamming equipment, and the picture of U.S. military aid to Haiti is largely complete.[29] Aid was $390,000 for the Haitian navy in 1983 compared with $9 million for the Dominican Republic.[30]

It is true the regime uses U.S. official and private influence for its own benefit, and the government seems to be increasingly dependent on American aid and multilateral loans to survive. For the time being, it survives mainly because it is anchored in Haitian political traditions. The president might well claim, in the language of the wily but weak character of Haitian oral literature who constantly escapes his enemies: "the day you catch Ti-Malice has not yet dawned."[31]

In the future, however, several factors may result in an increase in U.S. interest in Haiti. First is the growing political strength and international involvement of black Americans. Second, is the probable political organization of the nearly 5 million Americans of Caribbean origins, including Jamaicans, Dominicans, Haitians, Cubans, and others.[32] Immigration issues and foreign affairs concerns may bring about black American and Caribbean-American coalitions, with possible additional support from religious groups and others. The national debate in the 1980s over the plight of the Haitian boat people was an early indicator of possible future coalitions.

DEPENDENCE ON EXTERNAL ASSISTANCE

Another portent of the future is increasing dependence on the outside world. The worsening trade deficit, the steady decline of agriculture, and the end of mining as sources of revenue, and the unavailability of private capital for loans have altogether created a crisis of new proportions for Haiti's urban governing elites. In 1981, 23 percent of total national food consumed was imported,[33] and many of these imports were consumed by residents of Port-au-Prince. The annual disappearance of possibly one-third of government revenues into the pockets of the ruling family and government officials leaves limited money for development, debt servicing, or normal operations of government.[34] In 1981 Haiti's external debt stood at U.S. $277.3 million with annual interests payments of $17.8 million; its trade deficit reached $185,600,000. This situation has revived a debate about the goals and benefits of foreign aid among Haitians as well as among donor countries and agencies.

Particularly supportive of continuing high levels of U.S. aid are American business people in Port-au-Prince, USAID officials, and the Haitian government. The latter needs foreign assistance to ensure continuing ability to pay salaries. Foreign investors and traders consider foreign aid an invaluable to business. USAID officials and consultants believe aid can help. They also benefit from high salaries and consulting fees. The amount of money spent by American taxpayers in Haiti is more modest than in other countries, and for several years of Dr. Duvalier's rule U.S. assistance was negligible. Aimé Césaire, the French Martinican leader and writer, puts bitter complaints in the mouths of the Haitian protagonists in his play *La Tragédie du Roi Christophe:* they say the only aid the country received after independence was a master of ceremonies for King Christophe's court.[35] It has certainly increased since those days, but the Dominican Republic regularly receives from one and a half to two times more U.S. economic assistance than Haiti. Since the 1980 change of government, Jamaica receives almost three times more assistance than Haiti even though it has less than one-third the population. Private organizations using U.S. government money spend more elsewhere, too: the Inter-American Foundation spent $1.7 million in Haiti from 1971 to 1980 compared with $3.4 million in the Dominican Republic for the same period.[36]

The government of Jean-Claude Duvalier has mastered the techniques of the weak in dealing with the strong to obtain and control aid. Secrecy, evasion, intimidation of individuals, apparent compliance without implementation, patience in waiting for a change in aid personel, exploiting the fear of communism, and effective use of informal means of communication are the techniques that "Ti-Malice" would also use to ensure his survival in the world of "Bouqui," the strong but gullible character in Haitian Creole literature. A poignant example of intimidation was reported by the press in 1980. When the head of USAID in Haiti raised questions during a meeting of donor countries with the government of Haiti about the deterioration of respect for human rights, a bell-wielding Haitian minister silenced him contemptuously. After being admonished, the U.S. official obediently continued the discussion along more "technical" lines as the minister instructed him to do.[37]

Current American bilateral aid to Haiti fluctuates around $30 million a year about half of which is in the form of food under the Food for Peace or PL 480 program. West Germany was second to the United States in 1980 with a program worth $9 million. Then came France with $7.3 million (up from $1.2 million in 1979) and Canada with $5.3 million. Other countries accounted for $6.3 million,[38] including Israel, which has provided agricultural help. Great Britain has no bilateral aid program; nor is there a resident British ambassador, although there are diplomatic relations. International or multilateral agencies, whose single largest contributor is the United States, have made significant commitments to Haiti. The World Bank's program in 1981 amounted to $33.9 million. Its low interest fund or IDA committed $3.2 million in 1981 compared with $18.5 million in 1979, and the IDB (Inter-American Development Bank) allocated $9.1 million in 1981 compared with $38.3 million in 1979.[39] Haiti receives no assistance from communist or OPEC countries. It is not now included in the arrangements made by Mexico and Venezuela for concessional aid to oil consumers.

After the provision of food, the most important U.S. programs have been in what is called an integrated agriculture, rural development, and nutrition project. Construction and maintenance of secondary or gravel roads is the most important aspect. In addition, however, this money is allocated for potable water projects, reforestation, which is just beginning, and rural credit services. The U.S. Caribbean Basin Initiative is supposed to provide an extra $10 million for Haiti, half of which will go for loans to labor intensive industries; $4 million will go to private voluntary organizations, and $1 million to the government for technical studies to be undertaken by the Ministry of Planning and others. USAID continues to try to encourage American private investors through an Office of Private Enterprise Development.

American aid efforts in Haiti have been subject over the years to sharp criticisms from within and outside the U.S. government. In early 1982 the General Accounting Office published a negative evaluation of the U.S. aid program. The GAO took a clear position with respect to the responsibility of the Haitian government for aid failures.[40] The report urged that more American money be channeled through private voluntary organizations which are less obliged to deal with the government than is a U.S. government agency. The U.S. House of Representatives' Committee on Foreign Affairs sent a study mission to the island in April 1981, and its members also concluded that "to the maximum extent possible, U.S. assistance to Haiti should be furnished through non-governmental channels."[41] These reports had some effect on USAID: In its 1983 presentation to Congress its representatives asserted very clearly they were serving the strategic interests of the United States through their programs in Haiti. Further, they stated that over 50 percent of USAID projects were already being carried out by private organizations.

The low opinion of the Haitian government is shared by other donors such as the Canadian government and the Inter-American Development Bank. Canadian legislators have also recommended "that a larger share of the funds allocated by the Canadian aid programme in Haiti should be directed toward non-governmental organizations." There are 130 private organizations of Canadian origin now working in Haiti.[42] PVOs themselves have joined the chorus. The Inter-American Foundation's Robert Maguire claimed that AID takes a "top-down approach" meaning that American government employees and Haitian government employees plan and administer programs for the rural poor who have little to say about them.[43] Maguire further concluded from his study of one AID project that it had reenforced government authority and had served the financial interests of one high official better than the interests of the peasants.[44]

General studies of Haiti show a continued downward drift in spite of these programs designed to help rural areas. The U.S. House of Representatives' staff study mission recommended termination of the Integrated Agricultural Development Program because, in their judgment, it is a failure.[45] In November 1981 the Canadian government very abruptly terminated its integrated regional program, with the acronym DRIPP, at Petit Goâve. One reason was that the Haitian officials took advantage of it to provide salaries to hundreds of people not productively associated with DRIPP. Another reason, as the Canadian's admit, was that the project was not well conceived by the Canadians themselves.[46]

All donors regularly engage in intense, internal discussions about Haiti. They all complain about the same problems of unkept promises, dissimulation, disappearing funds, and the inexorable rural decline. The highly respected Marc Bazin negotiated a loan of $37.6 million from the International Monetary Fund before his dismissal as Minister of Finance,[47] and his successor, Frantz Merceron, promised to implement the reforms demanded by the IMF. These reforms include removal of hundreds of persons from the public payroll, use of a computer to control receipts and disbursements for the tax office, customs office, and for salary payments. A Canadian firm is supposed to audit government books.[48] Channeling the aid through foreign PVO's reduces the risk of corruption but does nothing to improve or institutionalize the performance of the Haitian government. Yet road building seems to be one of the few activities which the Haitian government can carry out responsibly without serious corruption. Ironically road building was one of the few administrative capabilities developed during the U.S. occupation.

Road building and maintenance are important for Haiti. It is doubtless true that better roads can break the hold of richer peasants over the poor, permit access to schools and markets, and increase food supplies. Sociologist Uli Locher has estimated that 15 to 17 percent of food is wasted during transport because of poor roads.[49]

THE DEBATE OVER AID TO HAITI CONTINUES

Almost 20 years ago Leslie Manigat, a prominent black Haitian intellectual in exile, wrote that aid cutoffs could not adversely affect the government of Dr. Duvalier because Haitians could endure suffering.[50] Today, he, Georges Anglade and some other opponents of the regime outside the country currently oppose foreign aid because they believe that Jean-Claude Duvalier, who is less politically astute than his father, needs the aid to protect himself and the elites. In July 1982 high ranking civil servants wrote a letter to a representative of the United Nations in Haiti to urge the cessation of aid because of growing chaos in the country.[51] On the other hand, the authors of the very critical OAS report on human rights in Haiti recommended continuing aid. Other outside critics—Haitian and non-Haitian—are not united on the issue.

Observers point out that on a per capita basis the aid Haiti receives is comparatively low. Belize, with less than 200,000 people, received as much as Haiti, with almost 6 million people, under the Caribbean Basin Initiative of President Reagan. It is probably true that if Haiti had a better reputation, members of Congress, including the Black Caucus, and others would lobby more energetically for assistance to the republic. For the present it appears the primary concerns of the U.S. government are stability in Haiti and preventing the flow of illegal immigrants to North America. A sudden upheaval could bring to power persons antagonistic to U.S. interests in the Caribbean, and it is highly likely the Cubans would attempt to exert influence during a period of transition.

Because U.S. interests are so general, the Haitian government has considerable room to maneuver and manipulate Washington in the pursuit of its own well-defined and narrow interests. Seen in terms of the global competition between the United States and the Soviet Union, aid to Haiti has been successful thus far. Seen in terms of concrete and steady progress in political, administrative, or economic development for the people, aid to Haiti has not been successful.

While the aid discussions continue, international organizations, private groups, American public opinion and the U.S. government in particular are faced with a pressing problem posed by a massive migration out of Haiti into the Caribbean and toward the United States.

FLIGHT FROM HAITI:
EXILES, REFUGEES, AND MIGRANTS

Voluntary or forced exile has been the fate of many Haitian political leaders ever since the French captured Toussaint Louverture. Jamaica, Canada, the United States of America, and France were the usual destinations. There are now small communities of Haitian professionals, intellectuals, and former politicians in Cuba, Venezuela, and Africa as well. Stripping individuals of their Haitian citizenship, putting opponents on ships or airplanes, and requiring native born Haitians to obtain a visa to leave as well as to return to Haiti are some of the nonviolent ways the Duvalier family has protected itself from political opposition.

Haitians have long emigrated to seek temporary or permanent work. Between 1913 and 1930 nearly 300,000, mostly young men, were voluntarily recruited to work on Cuban sugar estates. Many were repatriated during the Great Depression—but geographer Georges Anglade believes there are now 250,000 persons of Haitian descent in Cuba.[52] Thousands also sought work in the Dominican Republic.

Since the 1950s Haitian legal and illegal emigration has been directed toward the United States, Canada, the Bahamas, and the Dominican Republic with smaller numbers reaching France and its Caribbean dependencies, and Africa. Rough estimates of the size of the Haitian diaspora in 1980 vary between 700,000 and 1 million or 10 to 14 percent of all Haitians.[53] Half are in the United States, and 200,000 are in the Dominican Republic. Another 25,000 are in Canada (mostly Quebec), 20,000 in French Guyana, and possibly 25,000 live in the Bahamas. Several thousand live in France, West Africa, and Venezuela.

This emigration has its advantages for the regime. It removes some political dissidents, brings remittances of perhaps $100 million a year, relieves land pressure and rural overcrowding, and slows down the growth of Port-au-Prince's urbanization. Some emigrants returned during the 1970s bringing investment capital and valuable skills, while others traveled back and forth from Haiti to their new homes.

The Haitian government treats emigration as a business. Taxes, expensive visas, and other fees were used to collect from those exiting legally while the tontons macoutes often harassed those leaving undocumented. However, as more and more governments shut their doors to emigrants in general and to Haitians in particular (the Bahamas), the government is becoming preoccupied with lack of access. It has tried and failed to negotiate migration agreements with Belize and other countries and has reluctantly accepted increased aid as a payoff for allowing U.S. ships to intercept boat people in Haitian waters.

Haitians emigrate for multiple reasons. Prospects of work, higher income, and further education mix with the desire to escape police and government harassment. It is a mistake to assume that a single motive prevails in most individual cases. As indicated, poor Haitians experience such acute poverty and generalized political oppression that their motives are several; it is difficult to separate economic and political reasons for the flight although it is not uncommon to hear Haitians say they will return once they have made enough money.

The 1980 U.S. Refugee Act uses the UN definition for asylum and refugee status. Refugees are persons with a justified fear of persecution due to their beliefs, race or ethnic group, if returned to their home country. Haitians have found it difficult to prove their refugee status to U.S. imigration officials, as have persons from other countries such as South Korea and the Philippines which have good relations with the United States.[54] Haitians have not qualified as refugees in Canada or France either except for a handful of intellectuals and politicians.

Since the 1960s Haitians have been emigrating, legally and illegally, at a rate of about 50,000 a year from all regions of the country and social classes. However, only in the early 1970s did Haitians rely on small and fragile boats to reach Florida from northwestern Haitian fishing villages; a two to three week perilous trip. Between 1974 and 1983 more than 40,000 Haitian boat people were apprehended coming ashore in Florida. Countless others were never caught or else died or drowned during the voyage.

The U.S. government, Florida authorities, and most Americans have been at a loss as to what to do with these Haitians who have risked their lives to reach American shores. Some boat people were cynically helped en route by Cuban officials who provided food and water. No other government anywhere in the world has shown an interest in receiving unskilled Haitians who have sold their possessions and borrowed at extortionate rates to pay for a dangerous trip. The question is whether they should be considered refugees and granted asylum, repatriated to Haiti, or allowed to enter the U.S. on some other basis, such as temporary legal migrants.

All arrivals without a proper visa and claiming asylum are supposed to have a hearing to determine their eligibility. The U.S. Immigration and Naturalization Service (INS) decided in 1978 to limit opportunities to present a case for political asylum when they were faced with a great increase in the asylum claim from Haitians and others. Speedy mass processing of Haitians consciously designed to facilitate deportation brought a strong reaction from church groups, lawyers, and human rights organizations. In an effort to prevent summary deportation lawyers began court action against the INS in 1979, and since that time the courts have ruled against the INS. In the case *Haitian Refugee Center* vs. *Civiletti*, lawyers claimed the INS program violated the Haitians' rights and that "the government has unfairly prejudged the Haitians' claims for political asylum."[55] After hearing the evidence from both sides federal judge James Lawrence King decided the INS had indeed violated the rights of the black boat people and ruled that it must process asylum applications according to its own rules. He also accepted the evidence presented that even if the Haitians did not originally leave as political exiles, their expected persecution upon returning home made a good case for considering them political exiles.

Immigration authorities followed the judge's instruction to process each case, but they began to intern Haitians entering after October 1980. About 2,000 were placed in detention facilities in Florida, Puerto Rico, New York, and elsewhere. The same church and human rights groups went back to the courts to seek relief while the press also condemned this action pointing out that Haitians applying for asylum were an insignificant number compared with more than 36,000 Cubans and 7,000 Iranians in 1981: "All told 63,202 foreigners asked for asylum" of which only 503 were Haitians.[56] In August 1982 Judge Eugene Spellman ruled that 1,800 Haitian internees must be released from camps in Florida and Puerto Rico into the custody of sponsors until their cases could be decided on an individual basis. This release on parole is no guarantee they will be allowed to remain permanently in the country. U.S. officials believe all these actions have stemmed the flow into the United States, and claim they can now prove Haitians are not persecuted when they return.

In Haiti a neat distinction between political interest and economic well being is virtually impossible to make. Those citizens without family or friendship ties with the army or the VSNs are defenseless if and when a soldier or a VSN wants to seize their land or abuse them. If one is relatively rich, these predators can be bought off. The Inter-American Commission on Human Rights of the Organization of American States confirmed "the large-scale seizure of peasant lands by Tonton Macoutes following any dispute or denunciation....''[57] The same is true for jobs in Port-au-Prince.

Any action or comment can be interpreted as a political statement against the regime, and then the individual is subject to the harshest repression. According to Judge King, "Not only is it illegal to talk bad about the government, but the criminal statutes are so broad and ambiguous as to encompass virtually any act (or thought).''[58] Thus, labor organizations have documented the arrest of workers at places such as HASCO sugar mill when they requested improved working conditions.[59] Other workers who have dared set up trade unions to improve their economic conditions have been beaten and arrested because the government considers this action to be a threat to its combined political and economic interests.[60]

The issue of race has been raised in the United States because black Haitians were the largest single group seeking asylum to be detained and for the longest time. Non-Haitians were also detained no matter what their color, but not in the same numbers as Haitians and not with the accompanying publicity. The advocates of the Haitian boat people criticized the Carter administration first for treating the Haitians differently from the Cubans who arrived in 1980 and who were, for the most part, paroled. Monsignor Bryan Walsh of the Roman Catholic church relief services testified before the Senate Committee on the Judiciary that the government could have also paroled Haitians as a group under the law as it existed in early 1980.[61] Congressman Walter E. Fauntroy criticized the Carter administration in stronger terms:

> We, as black people, want to make it clear that we understand the connection between treatment of the Haitian refugees and the regard which this administration may have for black people here at home. For the administration to fail to address this issue immediately in a humane and rational way by granting political refugee status by May 15, 1980, when the President's power to grant refugee status on a group basis to the Haitian boat people already in the United States expires, would condemn this administration as one of gross hypocrisy and racism.[62]

Reacting to this pressure, President Carter ordered INS officials to treat Haitians the same way it had been treating Cubans. Those who entered before October 10, 1980, were paroled, but those entering after that date were detained in the last months of the Carter administration and the first two years of the Reagan administration. After court action and public pressure, Haitians were released pending their hearings. In April 1983 the 11th U.S. Circuit Court of Appeals ruled the the federal government had discriminated against the Haitians when it incarcerated them in Florida and elsewhere. This ruling confirmed the accusations made by Congressman Fauntroy.

Tighter Canadian immigration laws and quotas, expulsion of Haitians from the Bahamas, U.S. measures to curb Haitian outflows, and similar steps elsewhere are having an impact. Minor outlets for Haitians in French Guyana or Guadeloupe and Martinique cannot make up the difference. Blocking emigration may have a dramatic impact on Haiti. This topic is discussed further in the next chapter.

Hundreds of thousands of Haitians will doubtless continue to try to enter the United States illegally. Repatriating those who came by boat and turning back other Haitian ships will place the emphasis on other, probably more expensive methods of illegal entry. The proposed 1983 U.S. immigration legislation would sanction American employers who knowingly hire illegal aliens. It is of limited import to Haitian illegals who find marginal jobs in service and other low-cost sectors where U.S. law enforcement is weak. However, the 1983 proposals also expedite hearings for political asylum and strengthen the government's legal ability to detain those seeking asylum rather than granting them parole.

We believe that those Haitians who do seek refugee status should be granted open, fair, and speedy hearings and that while awaiting such hearings they should not be detained. We believe that the definition of what constitutes a refugee should be based on extensive empirical evidence of Haitian political life with an understanding that now much persecution by Haitian authorities particularly in rural areas is arbitrary, whether or not the individual in question has actually opposed the regime.

In short, during its 180 years of independence, Haiti's relations with the rest of the world have been often frustrating and problematical. Bonds of language and race have helped but isolation has persisted. In the 1980s the populace looks north for a better life, and Haitian leaders are also drifting into an increasing dependence on the United States which they have learned to manipulate but not to maximize. The lack of stable and beneficial relations with the rest of the world remains a grave problem. One of the many challenges of the last two decades of the twentieth century is for Haiti to improve its relations with the Dominican Republic and the other Caribbean states.

NOTES

1. Cited by Rayford W. Logan, *The Diplomatic Relations of the United States with Haiti, 1776–1891* (Chapel Hill: University of North Carolina, 1941), p. 178.

2. Cited by Hans Schmidt, *The United States Occupation of Haiti 1915–1934* (New Brunswick: Rutgers University Press, 1971), p. 142.

3. *The Life and Writing of Frederick Douglass, Vol. IV: Reconstruction and and After* (New York: International, 1955), p. 485.

4. "Editorial," in *The Crisis* (September 1915):232.

5. Congressional Black Caucus Task Force on Haitian Refugees, "Statement of Purpose Fact-Finding Mission to Haiti," Washington, D.C., 30 June 1982.

6. Christian Filostrat, "The Search for an African Identity in the Caribbean: Genesis and Rise of Haitianism and Negritude" (Ph.D. diss., Howard University, Washington, D.C., 1978), p. 146.

7. Alain Yacou, "La conscience d'une menace impérialiste dans la presse haïtienne," *Bulletin de la Société d'Histoire de la Guadeloupe* nos. 45–46 (1980):83–111, and, Mercer Cook, "Trends in Recent Haitian Literature," *The Journal of Negro History* 32 (April 1947):230.

8. Hannibal Price, *De la réhabilitation de la Race Noire par la République d'Haïti* (Port-au-Prince: Verrollet, 1901), p. 153.

9. Ibid., p. 164.

10. Jean F. Brierre, "Me revoici Harlem," cited and trans. by Mercer Cook, "Trends in Recent Haitian Literature", p. 229.

11. F. Morisseau-Leroy, *Récolte* (Port-au-Prince: Les Editions Haïtiennes, 1946), p. 30.

12. 1959 speech by Jean Price-Mars, reprinted in *Conjonction*, no. 115, 1971, p. 57.

13. René Depestre, *Bonjour et adieu à la négritude* (Paris: Robert Laffont, 1980), p. 231.

14. Lorimer Denis and François Duvalier, *Evolution stadiale du Vodou* (Port-au-Prince: Imprimerie de l'Etat, 1944, Publication du Bureau d'Ethnologie de la République d'Haïti, no. 3), p. 28.

15. Jean Price-Mars, *Lettre ouverte au Dr. René Piquion sur son manuel de la négritude, Le préjugé de couleur est-il la question sociale?* (Port-au-Prince: Editions des Antilles, 1967), p. 33.

16. *Le Petit Samedi Soir*, 14–20 August 1982, p. 5.

17. "Report of the Commission of Inquiry . . . ." (Geneva: ILO, 1983), p. 107.

18. We are depending here on the forthcoming book by Mats Lundahl, *Man, Land and Markets: Essays on the Haitian Economy*, (London and Canberra: Croom Helm, 1983).

19. *Le Monde Diplomatique*, August 1982, p. 10.

20. See *Haiti Observateur*, 4–11 March 1983, p. 2.

21. For a different view see Suzy Castor, *La ocupación northeamericana de Haití y sus consecuencias (1915–1934)* (Mexico: Siglo Veintiuno, 1971), pp. 199–211.

22. Ernst Verdieu, "Entre le Canada et Haïti des échanges économiques éloquents," *Le Devoir* (Montreal), 9 December 1980, p. 11.

23. See Anthony Ramirez, "Haiti's Fiscal Woes Deter Investment," in *Wall Street Journal,* 15 August 1980, p. 19. For some American business opinion see U.S., Congress, House, "Hearings before the Subcommittee on Inter-American Affairs of the Committee on Foreign Affairs," 97th Cong., 1st sess., 28 April 1981, p. 51.

24. Robert A. Pastor, "Our Real Interests in Central America," in *The Atlantic Monthly,* July 1982, p. 35.

25. Edwin M. Martin, "Haiti: A Case Study in Futility," in *SAIS Review,* Summer 1981, pp. 61–70.

26. *Haiti-Observateur,* 3–10 September 1982, p. 1.

27. *Le Monde,* 24 March 1982, p. 4., and, "Seafaring FBI Says It Foils 15 Set for Haiti," in *The Washington Post,* 18 March 1982, p. A19.

28. Reported by *Haïti-Observateur,* 21–28 May 1982, p. 9.

29. Robert Debs Heinl, Jr. and Nancy Gordon Heinl, *Written in Blood: The Story of the Haitian People: 1492–1971* (Boston: Houghton Mifflin, 1978), pp. 656, 659–60.

30. *Haïti-Observateur,* 21–28 May 1982, p. 9.

31. Suzanne Comhaire-Sylvain, *Le roman de Bouqui,* (Port-au-Prince: Imprimerie Collège Vertières, 1940), p. 69.

32. See Pastor, "Our Real Interests," pp. 37–39.

33. Christian Girault, presentation at symposium, "Haiti: Present State and Future Prospects," Wingspread Foundation, Racine, Wisconsin, 23–26 September 1982.

34. The figure of 36 percent was suggested by Bazin. See *Le Monde,* 4 May 1982, p. 4.

35. Aimé Césaire, *La tragédie du Roi Christophe* (Paris: Presence Africaine, 1963).

36. "Hearings and Markup Before the Subcommittee on Inter-American Affairs of the Committee on Foreign Affairs," March 23, 26, 30, April 8, 1981. (Washington: GPO, 1981), pp. 21–22.

37. *Washington Post,* 21 December 1980, p. A25.

38. Agency for International Development, "Congressional Presentation for Haiti—Fiscal Year 1983," p. 175.

39. Ibid.

40. United States General Accounting Office, *Assistance to Haiti: Barriers, Recent Program Changes and Future Options* (Washington: GAO, ID 82–13, February 22, 1982), p. 1.

41. "Memorandum to Members of the Committee on Foreign Affairs," from John J. Brady, Jr., Chief of Staff, 6 May 1981, p. 1.

42. Standing Committee on External Affairs and National Defense, *Canada's Relations with the Caribbean and Central America: Report to the House of Commons* 29 July 1982, (Hull, Quebec: Canadian Government Publishing Centre,

1982), p. 27. George Anglade says there are now so many foreign aid experts in Haiti "that the average Haitian family is composed of parents, grandparents, children and a foreign development expert." *Espace et liberté en Haïti* (Montreal: ERCE and CRC, 1982), p. 82.

43. Robert Maguire, *Bottom-Up Development in Haiti* 2nd ed. (Rosslyn, Va: Inter-American Foundation, April 1981), pp. 16-17.

44. Ibid., p. 18. For the AID view of their program see USAID/Haiti, *Country Program Overview* (Port-au-Prince and Washington: AID, October 1982).

45. "Memo to Members of Committee of Foreign Affairs," p. 2.

46. Standing Committee, *Canada's Relations with the Caribbean*, pp. 25-26. DRIPP means Développement régional intégeré de Petit-Goâve et de Petit-trou-de-Nippes.

47. "IMF Agrees to Lend Haiti $37.6 Million," in *Wall Street Journal*, 11 August 1982, p. 26.

48. See Richard J. Meislin, "Donors Press Haiti on Use of Aid Funds," in *New York Times*, 12 September 1982, p. 3.

49. Uli Locher, sociologist, remarks at symposium, "Haiti: Present State and Future Prospects," Wingspread Foundation, Racine, Wisconsin, 23-26 September 1982.

50. Leslie F. Manigat, *Haiti of the Sixties: Object of International Concern*, (Washington: The Washington Center for Foreign Policy Research, 1964), p. 91.

51. Reported in *Haïti-Observateur*, 20-27 August 1982, pp. 1, 9.

52. Georges Anglade, Denis Audette, Rafael Emilio Yunen, *Hispaniola: Les lectures d'une carte murale* (Montréal: Université de Québec, 1982).

53. Laënnec Hurbon, "Un peuple en fuite," in *Le Monde Diplomatique*, August 1982, p. 12.

54. Alex Stepick with Dale Frederick Swartz, *Haitian Refugees in the U.S.* (London: Minority Rights Group, 1982), pp. 12-13. Also his "Haitian Boat People: Both Economic and Political Refugees," *Law and Comtemporary Problems* 45 (1982).

55. Stepick, *Haitian Refugees in the U.S.*, p. 14.

56. Editorial, "A Haitian Freeze," in *New York Times*, 18 December 1981, p. 30.

57. *Report of the Situation of Human Rights in Haiti*, OEA/Ser.L/V/11.46, (Washington: General Secretariat OAS, 1979), p. 73.

58. *503 Federal Supplement 442*, (Southern District Florida), 1980, 2 July 1980, p. 502.

59. "News Release," U.S. Relations Office, Central Latinoamericana de Trabajadores, 14 November 1980.

60. Confédération Mondiale du Travail, "Memorandum de la CMT sur la Situation à Haiti," January 1981, p. 4.

61. U.S., Congress, Senate, Committee on the Judiciary, *Caribbean Refugee Crisis: Cubans and Haitians*, 96th Cong., 2nd sess., 12 May 1980, p. 16.

62. Ibid., p. 54.

6

CHALLENGES AND RESPONSES

According to peasant storytellers, "Ti-Malice" meets his end igno-miniously. He who has tricked so many is himself convinced to cut off his head in the mistaken belief he can then be in two places at once.[1] The threats to Haiti as a viable state and nation are also self-inflicted wounds. They take the form of both internal challenges that threaten the bases of the society and responses which are inadequate for national survival. Like "Ti-Malice," Haiti is engaged in self-destruction.

The principal challenges to the nation are five. The first is ecological because of deforestation and soil erosion. The second is demographic due to population growth and rapid urbanization in and around Port-au-Prince. The third is social and includes massive migration and the continuing brain drain of professionals and technicians. The fourth is economic, meaning growth is too slow or negative while income and service are unfairly distributed. Fifth there is politics with its stagnant, self-serving leadership patterns. The five are closely related in causal chains. The failure of politicians to help peasants arrest soil erosion accelerates rural to urban and overseas migration; it also impedes any hope of rural growth and worsens rural-urban disparities while undermining traditional culture. Widespread mutual distrust inhibits collective responses, and inadequate or inappropriate responses intensify the illness. Doing something is not necessarily better than doing nothing in Haiti, but doing nothing is to concede defeat.

ECOLOGICAL CHALLENGES

The most demanding and difficult of all problems are the ecological. An exporter of mahogany and other hardwoods for centuries, Haiti is now 90 percent denuded. There are no effective forest reserves or other protected areas and only a handful of badly paid and trained forest rangers to protect the entire country. Commercial lumbering ceased in the early twentieth century, and urban Haiti must now import both combustible fuels and building materials.

Lacking the funds to purchase kerosene or other imported fuels, Haitian peasants rely on collected brush, brambles, saplings, and other forest products for firewood and charcoal. Their fuel needs include warmth for cold mountain nights, cooking, distilling sugarcane juice, and illumination. Their steady encroachment on steep, already partly denuded slopes, is the main cause of deforestation, not commercial offtake.[2] Insignificant and unenforced sanctions are minimal deterrents as they go further and further in their pursuit of fuel. Relentless deforestation was a minor problem in the nineteenth century when many forested areas remained, but it has become a direct threat to the livelihood of most Haitians. Haiti's tropical rains sweep the topsoil off the deforested hillsides and leave the scar of gullies and ravines. According to one estimation, for every annual 5 percent loss in forest the country loses 6,000 more hectares of topsoil.[3] An aerial view of Haiti looks like a bald and deeply creased skull. The land has become permanently maimed, and marine life has been adversely affected by the tons of soil flowing into the Caribbean.

This erosion is also the result of growing land shortage. As rural populations mount, and farms become more fragmented, arable land is over worked, fallow periods are shortened, livestock is allowed to graze in fallow land destroying the regenerative cycle, and marginal land is cultivated. The soil becomes quickly exhausted, especially where it is light, sandy, and friable. Cultivation without terracing puts further stress on hillsides. Terracing is not regularly practiced in Haiti except in a few areas.

Deforesting and soil erosion may have already carried off 20 percent of Haiti's total potentially arable land.[4] Construction of proposed hydroelectric projects will remove more land from cultivation in the Artibonite Valley. According to 210 Canadian missionaries working in Haiti, who signed a letter addressed to their prime minister, 1100 hectares will be lost in the region of La Chapelle and 2,750 in the region of Verrettes.[5] At an estimated rate of loss of 1 percent of arable land a year, Haiti risks mass starvation conditions before the end of the century. The ecological problems constitute a national emergency. What has been the response?

ECOLOGICAL RESPONSES

The Haitian government in its public pronouncements recognizes the seriousness of these ecological problems, but it does no more than to create urban offices staffed by sinecures "in defense of soil conservation." It could choose one of three options. One would be to use forced labor to mobilize rural Haitians to undertake reforestation and antierosion works, but this would recall forced labor under the U.S. occupation and would necessitate administrative skills which are lacking. The second would be through ideology, nationalism, and other noncoercive forms of persuasion to mobilize the rural population, but the government prefers a denuded countryside to an aroused peasantry. The third option would be to use cash or trees as incentives to carry out the works, and this is what the previously mentioned USAID pilot project is doing now. Support for reforestation has also come from Congressman Clarence Long who carefully watches aid programs and who visits the country frequently to study the deforestation problems.

U.S. congressional interest is important since ecological factors are related to migration to the United States. Push factors forcing farmers off the land are powerful in Haiti, and erosion is among the foremost. There can be little doubt that the failure to respond to the ecological challenge will swell the number of rural Haitians voting with their feet.

DEMOGRAPHIC CHALLENGES

Haiti's demographic problems are equally pressing. They are population increase, high rural density, the youth of the population, and the overly rapid urbanization of the capital. Emigration is for some a problem and for others an opportunity.

Haiti has had censuses in 1950, 1971, and 1982. The censuses of 1950 and 1971 relied on a 10 percent rural sample and a 100 percent urban sampling, and they are replete with methodological, reporting, and other errors.[6] Civil registers are inadequate, scarcely registering urban data and missing the rural areas. Thus, there is no national information on births or deaths. The 1982 census, conducted in Creole and French, and prepared carefully, should provide more useful data when it is published.

It is already known that death due to curable or preventable illness is the primary check on population growth. The most detailed study of fertility and mortality was carried out in 1967–73 by a U.S. medical missionary couple.[7] Their sample of 9,000 persons was drawn from 23 villages located near the famous Schweitzer Hospital, a private, nonprofit venture

80 miles north of Port-au-Prince. Their study did not use hospital attendance as a control but it is probable that hospital facilities are better in this
rural area than elsewhere. This study estimated annual infant mortality at
140 deaths per 1000 live births and fertility at 34–36 live births annually
per 1000 women in the ages of fecundity (15–48). Other estimates are even
worse, and suggest that Haitian life expectancy is the lowest in the Western
Hemisphere. Fertility is probably reduced due to the incidence of venereal
disease, lactation between pregnancies, malnutrition resulting in miscar-
riages, and other factors. It is substantially below the 40–50 live births per
thousand found in some African countries. However, this reduction is not
due to the practice of abortion, contraception, infanticide, or other measures. Poor health results in Haitian women having fewer children than
they wish. A partly related factor may be the absence of adult males who
are seeking work in the Dominican Republic or elsewhere.

The infant mortality figures for Haiti are among the highest in the
world. Malnutrition, intestinal diseases, respiratory dieases including tuber-
culosis, tetanus, typhoid, measles, and other illnesses are all child-killers
in Haiti. Yaws is the only contagious disease to have been largely eliminated by a national public health campaign in the 1950s with U.S. and UN
aid. The other diseases occur and are perpetuated in the absence of ele-
mentary rural health facilities and programs.

Haiti's population composition and distribution are also problems. The
1971 census estimated 40 percent of the population as being 14 years of
age or younger.[8] This figure indicates the order of magnitude of the
young persons needing places in school, employment, or land, and other
social services. It also suggests the continued potential for high fertility
in a young population likely to marry and initiate child bearing early. No
census data were collected on racial composition, which is said to be 5
percent mulatto.

Haiti's estimated population density of 700 persons per square kilometer of arable land is one of the highest in the world, The semiarid northwest had a lower density but otherwise the rural population distribution
is relatively even. All regions are contributing to the rapid growth of the
Port-au-Prince metropolitan area. In 1971 the estimated population of the
capital was 501,825.[9] The 1982 census should show that the population
is soaring to about 1 million. Uli Locher, a sociologist at McGill University, estimates that by the year 2000 about 50 percent of Haiti's population will be in the area of Port-au-Prince, that is, between the suburb of
Carrefour to the west and the town of Croix des Bouquets to the east.[10]
Thus, migration out of the country will not offset this internal flow for
which the capital is totally unprepared.

DEMOGRAPHIC RESPONSES

Awareness of Haitian population problems is found in the 1949 Report of the UN Technical Assistance Mission, which recommended mass emigration. No family planning programs were initiated until the mid-1960s when several external religious and nonprofit organizations took quiet initiatives. Family planning was suspect during the reign of President François Duvalier. It was not until 1973 that Jean-Claude Duvalier publically spoke of demographic problems and endorsed and legitimized family planning. The Haitian government was anxious to obtain external donor support for its own family planning programs and was awarded with funding from the UN. Other donors and nonprofit groups were made subject to the authority of the Ministry of Health and a slow and cumbersome bureaucratic process.[11]

No more than 5–10 percent of Haitian women of childbearing age could be said to be practicing family planning by the early 1980s. This includes urban elites and other women relying on over-the-counter purchases of pills or the advice of private physicians. The handful of government and nonprofit clinics are mostly in the capital, serving middle-income women. The few rural efforts have showed little interest unless family planning is combined with maternal and child health, nutrition, and other measures. Haitian mothers, expecting to lose one or more of every five children born, are hesitant to limit conception. Children are needed for farm labor, to provide for their elders at later ages, and for other reasons. The government has proposed making family planning accessible to 100 percent of women of childbearing age by the year 2000 but this makes little sense except as part of a national public health program. However, responding to lack of land and other rural pressures, Haitian women are showing signs of reducing fertility, according to some observers.

The official response to problems of population distribution has been to aggravate them. Seemingly fearing the growth of independent political centers, especially in the traditional northern stronghold of Cap Haïtien, the government systematically impeded the growth of Cap and other secondary cities. Dr. Duvalier's refusal to pave roads, improve ports, extend airstrips, authorize hotels, and other measures had been used to direct development toward the capital. The monopoly of export trade in particular was used to ensure Port-au-Prince's primacy. Under Jean-Claude Duvalier foreign assistance has improved roads considerably, and there is talk of regional development, particularly around Cap Haitiene, Les Cayes, and Gonaïves. Proposed regional institutions would engage in planning economic development and encourage investments. It is too early to conclude it will be successful, but the regionalization is worth watching. Foreign aid officials are encouraging this project, as they should.

THE HAITIAN DIASPORA

The $100 million a year in remittances from Haitians abroad are important for Haiti. Observers estimate that the money from one Haitian worker employed in North America can feed and clothe four Haitians at home. The government through taxes, postal money order charges, and other devices takes several millions off the remittance—reportedly 3 gourdes or $0.60 for every $20 postal money order, for example. As a result, Haitians living abroad try to send remittances through travelers rather than through the banks and post offices. However it arrives, money from Haitians abroad helps keep almost a million Haitians alive. President Jean-Claude Duvalier has personally convinced selected Haitian technocrats abroad to return to prestigious and lucrative government posts. Some have accepted, few have remained, but the government cultivates its "open" image to the diaspora. However, unlike the Dominican Republic, there have been no fiscal or other incentives to induce the diaspora to invest at home, or schemes to take advantage of technicians willing to return for a short stay but not permanently.

The diaspora represents potentially one of Haiti's most valuable resources. Although most skilled Haitians abroad would not permanently return, under appropriate conditions many would invest and provide technical help. In many fields such as medicine there are more trained Haitians overseas than in Haiti. Their cultural attachments are strong, and their skills can be utilized.

Emigration is a personal rather than a national response in Haiti. Unlike Puerto Rico and the French and Netherlands Antilles, Haitians enjoy no preferential entry to any other country. Legally at best 25,000 Haitians a year can emigrate, taking advantage of the 20,000 a year U.S. ceiling identical for all countries and the few openings in Canada and France. Invariably those who emigrate legally are the best-educated and most resourceful. The government acknowledges this by the steep nuisance taxes it imposes on their departure. It can be argued that the stagnant Haitian economy cannot absorb its skilled manpower and that the country benefits from their higher earnings abroad and remittances. This may well be the case, but Haiti invested scarce resources in their education and training which are only partly reimbursed. The drama comes in the illegal status of many migrants, the high risk conditions of their departure and return, and the frightful conditions under which they work abroad. Their willingness to take their chances on small boats, in lands as distant as French Guyana, and for pitifuly low wages, is a testimony to their spirit and endurance and to the hardships of Haitian poverty.

Legal and illegal Haitian emigration is significantly reducing the rate of population growth. Net emigration of perhaps 50,000 persons a year since the 1960s has been bringing down population increase from 2 to 1.5 percent annually.[12] This is a valuable relief for an overstressed economy and society. However, since it is mostly adult males who leave, the skewed age distribution of Haiti is reinforced. The Haitian government can prevent or delay departures but it has no control or even influence over possible countries of reception. It can do little to encourage emigration as a matter of policy. Its principal concern has been to extract revenue from those leaving and those abroad. A report to the International Labor Office estimates that Dominicans pay the Haitian government almost $250,000 per year for migrant workers.[13] Meanwhile net emigration probably keeps slowly deteriorating Haitian standards of living from falling more rapidly.

THE CHALLENGE OF ECONOMIC GROWTH

Haiti is one of the poorest countries in the world, but it is not in a hopeless situation. Its assets include a remarkably enterprising population including astute women traders and wholesalers, a vibrant culture reflected in arts and crafts, the widespread and legitimated value of private property, almost universal involvement with private markets and a monetary economy, a strong desire for education, and a geographic location in the Caribbean with easy access to North America and neighboring islands. Haiti has failed to achieve rapid or sustained economic growth, but it is not condemned in perpetuity to grinding poverty. While it cannot attain North American or Western European standards of living, it should be able to decently feed, clothe, and shelter its people as its equally densely populated neighbor, Barbados, has done. The obstacles are primarily political, not economic.

During the first 150 years of its independence Haiti's monetary economy fluctuated with the world price of coffee and the portion of that price its elites allowed the producers. Since the 1950s the elites have placed more of their hopes for growth in tourism, the enticement of assembly industries, and recently in industrial import substitution based on protection. These hopes are reflected in spending in North America on tourist promotion and the attempt to promote a "peaceful, stable, and safe" image, the passing of a series of incentives to attract foreign investors, and recently the investment of public funds in a series of economically dubious local industry projects. Since about 1970 the rise in the prices of food crops has attracted urban-based speculators who buy and sell rice, flour, and sugar. Unlike their ancestors, they are becoming interested in accumulating land to produce these commodities. This in turn forces peasants from the land. They become agricultural laborers or migrants to Port-au-Prince and eventually to Florida.[14]

These processes are uncontrolled by the government which has not had a coherent economic growth strategy. The several government efforts at official economic planning have resulted in feeble documents of little merit or interest and negligible impact.[15] Tourism and assembly industries have benefited from some improvements in government flexibility and performance although rigidities, bureaucracy, and delay remain problems.

There has probably not been a coherent Haitian approach to economic growth based on promotion of agriculture since King Henri Christophe. For those.on the land there are not enough agronomists and agricultural technicians to help them—unless Haitian experts in exile return home.

The government of Jean-Claude Duvalier has officially recognized the priority due to agriculture, but "strategy" reduces itself to asking external donors to fund rural secondary roads and maintenance, a few farm schools, and reforestation efforts. The elites are indifferent to peasant agricultural practices and yields. Insofar as they are becoming interested in agriculture, as indicated, it is the markets that draw their attention and owning land. The outcome is continuing agricultural stagnation, which drags down the entire economy.

Income is also extremely unevenly distributed in the republic—much more so than land. As already noted, 8,000 families have average annual income in excess of $54,000, concentrate about 44 percent of national income, and pay in direct taxes only 3.5 percent of their income. These figures set the dimensions of the income distribution problem which the government refuses to admit exists. Although it recognizes ecological, population, and slow growth problems, social justice and equity are not part of the official vocabulary, even for purposes of rhetoric.

Gross economic leveling or equalization in Haiti is not the issue; it would be of minimal economic value. There simply is not enough to redistribute in relation to national needs. Currently, 75 percent of Haitians live in absolute proverty; the nation falls 25 percent short of meeting its minimum food needs. Redistribution on a massive scale from the top 1 or 5 percent would not go very far. It would probably deprive the nation of vital human resources and dry up much private savings.

ECONOMIC RESPONSES

There are two alternative approaches to the problem of income distribution. Foreign aid donors have for several years been pressing the government to reform the administration, properly collect the corporate and income taxes, and account for all monies collected. This should permit a reduction in the export taxes, especially on coffee, and a greater return to producers. The government has submitted to these suggestions when it has been forced to do so in order to obtain IMF loans and other aid. Fiscally, Haiti could, by shifting toward direct taxes, reducing some of the indirect taxes, and investing the Régie profits, add perhaps $20–25 million a year to public sector funds available for the budget. It could improve and extend rural services and offer low-interest loans to farmers. The critical assumptions are that tax collection administration can be reformed, that new funds would be used for development, and that the government would be willing to risk losing the political support of money lending middlemen.

Another approach maintains that the government is irretrievably disorganized, corrupt, and uninterested in poor people. Therefore it should be induced to leave the farmers alone wherever possible and allow the churches and voluntary organizations, with donor support, to be responsible for most rural services. This approach would seek a reduction in the coffee and other export taxes, and an end to local market and other nuisance taxes on peasants. Private voluntary organizations (PVOs) would be given a governmental green light to extend their rural activities with a minimum of government interference. Since the best rural schools and farm projects are usually already privately run this approach would assume that the government has little of benefit to offer most Haitians and should keep out of the way. The Haitian rural potential for self-help cannot be mobilized by a government seen as hostile but can be tapped by organizations that have the confidence of peasants.

These PVOs are seeking ways to help improve the economy. Foreign governments' aid agencies and multilateral organizations seem sincerely interested in finding ways to enlarge their economic programs. However, press reports that food given to Haiti under PL–480 programs is regularly sold and even makes its way to markets in Florida is only one example of the weaknesses of aid programs. And, it undermines the willingness of donors to expand their efforts. It is difficult not to agree with the

American journalist who wrote that "There is little evidence that foreign aid has significantly improved the lives of poor Haitian peasants."[16]

Internally, widespread populism has not manifested itself in rural or urban Haiti since the suppression of Charlemagne Péralte's antioccupation movement. Agitation in the Artibonite Valley, and the 1983 peasant attack on authorities killing diseased pigs at Aquin have been fleeting and isolated thus far. Except for religion there are no national rural or urban organizations in Haiti, no peasant leagues, no young farmers groups, viable independent trade unions, political parties, no associations of coffee producers.

The hope is always there. Novelist Jacques Roumain sought in his work to evoke sentiments of rural self-help and populism. Manuel, his most memorable character, returns from many years of cane cutting in Cuba with new ideas to liberate his people. He is killed by the forces of ignorance and superstition, but his idea for an irrigation system lives on. His death unites the feuding "habitants," and through water control and unity the people are saved. Annaise, his pregnant widow, knows their child will see a better Haiti. It is possible there is such populist leadership waiting to emerge, especially among women traders, who lose money through rural decline and competition with urban-based speculators in food. These black women and their male counterparts buying coffee doubtless have strong ambitions for a better life. It is difficult to imagine any significant economic change which might satisfy the ambitions of this element without an alteration of the political system.

POLITICAL CHALLENGES

Whatever its failings with respect to demographic, ecological, and economic challenges, the Duvalier family regime has been a stunning success at political control through the franchise system. It has held power longer than any other regime in Haitian history. It has managed the vexing perennial Haitian problem of political succession by establishing a family dynasty, the first in Haitian history. It has utilized a flexible form of coercion and cooption, carrot and stick, in order to rule, although it has consistently been a repressive regime. It has deftly played the armed forces off against the tontons macoutes to reduce the military threat. It has shackled and then coopted the principal interest groups. It has extracted funds and talent from the Haitian diaspora while closely monitoring their political behavior, and it has carried out a foreign policy which has minimized threats and obtained some benefits from Haiti's most important diplomatic associates: the United States, the Dominican Republic, France, and Canada, as well as others.

The question of political control hangs on the nature of power and authority. Since 1957, the Duvaliers have relied on rubber-stamp elections and referendums without opposition of any kind to force through the presidency for life and other measures.[17] Passivity and fear are their greatest allies, but selected groups under Dr. Duvalier and then his son have benefited from the regime, and they support it.

The Duvaliers have sought to project an image of an isolated Haiti valiantly defending itself against hostile external forces. François Duvalier's calls to black Haitian nationalism and the spirit of the ancestors were frequent in a paranoiac regime which saw United Nations technical assistance as a potential plot. Jean-Claude Duvalier is much more comfortable with the external world and mulattoes and has less occasion to preach strident nationalism and racism. They are present, however, in the references to the Haitian revolution, to the glorious ancestors, and to the need to be constantly on guard against those foreign elements who would compromise Haitian sovereignty. The "defense of national interests," and "black interests," no matter how poorly they are actually defended, is the grand mystification, the ultimate bastion on which any Haitian government can seek to justify itself.

The leading question is the future of the Duvalier regime itself. Because Jean-Claude Duvalier came to office as a 19 year-old in 1971, he could conceivably still be alive in 2030. Since the birth of his son in 1983, the possibility exists of a third generation of Duvalier family presidents and another peaceful succession of power. This option seems most unlikely, however. Another 20 years in office as a minimum would be needed to produce and train a suitable heir. Whether through personal boredom on the part of the incumbent, family feuds, palace factions and intrigues, or external events, the odds are against the Duvalier regime being able to control the next succession. The internal economic and ecological challenges are too pressing and the influence of the growing diaspora is too large to permit a further lengthy period in office. The existence of a life presidency is an open invitation to all opponents to seek to terminate the regime while providing them with a minimum common platform. Changes in the constitution in August 1983 providing for succession of Jean-Claude Duvalier raised suspicions that the president might soon be replaced from within ruling circles. Articles 107, 108, 109 allow the president to name his successor and to designate a temporary replacement from among the cabinet ministers if he becomes ill. The fact that the successor and the temporary replacement may be different persons opens the door to conflict within the ruling group.

If the regime does not live out its days, how is it likely to be terminated? An unlikely possibility would be assassination followed by widespread public disorder. The president is well-protected, and his public appearances are unpredictable. Any act of assassination would require professionals willing to risk martyrdom. Most Haitians with that kind of training are already in the pay of the regime. Haitian history has been characterized by coups rather than assassinations with the important exceptions of the slaying of Dessalines in 1806 and of President Vilbrun Guillaume Sam in 1915. It is often said by Haitians themselves that they are too loquacious and boastful to maintain the secrecy needed in a carefully planned assassination and invasion, Dr. Price-Mars called it "verbomania."[18] Nor have some leaders in exile been able to judge accurately the reaction of peasants to their efforts. Depestre recalls listening with amazement in a Moscow hotel room as Dr. Jacques Stéphen Alexis claimed he could count on 40,000 Haitians to join him in seizing power in Port-au-Prince.[19] When Alexis did land on Haitian shores in April 1961, there was no uprising and no important support. Twenty years later Haitian-born Florida resident Bernard Sansariq convinced a small group of Haitians to follow him in a landing on the Ile de la Tortue where he promised hundreds of armed troops would join them. A provisional government would be established, and in due course it would replace the current regime. The whole affair would have been worthy of Gilbert and Sullivan if Sansaricq had not sent his advance party to their deaths.[20] In no case was there a peasant uprising to support these invasions.

Outside Haiti talented intellectuals in Venezuela lead the Rassemblement des Démocrates Nationaux et Progressistes (RDNP), whose secretary general is Leslie Manigat. The Hector Riobé Brigade based in Miami has succeeded in landing briefly by airplane, terrorizing a small group of people, and perhaps planning small random explosions which occurred.[21] Sansariq's Parti Populaire National Haïtien continues to recruit among exiles in Florida. Other groups such as the Parti Démocratique Haïtien operate in Canada, and the leading exile newspaper, Haïti-Observateur in New York calls for a unified opposition. None of these movements can seriously claim it has mass support or even an effective clandestine network within Haiti.

Also unlikely is a military coup. The army is partly disarmed with much of its arsenal in the presidential palace guarded by the loyal presidential guard. Dr. Duvalier stripped the army of its trained professional officers, both black and brown, replaced them with his own loyalists, and cut training and equipment to a minimum. The army of the 1930s that could drill smartly is no more. Understandably, all this could change, especially if younger officers, who now must have a high school diploma and attend courses in the law school, emerge anxious to establish a new role for the military. The power that the head of state exercises over all appointments is the regime's best defense against such thinking, but his reported susceptibility to flattery and sycophancy may allow enemies to infiltrate into important positions.

A successful coup or guerrilla war led by Haitian exiles is doubtful. Jamaica and the Dominican Republic are now unwilling to harbor active Haitian exile movements, and both the United States and Venezuela have arrested Haitians suspected of planning an invasion. One variant of the exile-led coup is a coup or guerrilla war backed by Cuba, but it would prompt a U.S. reaction, especially with U.S. Coast Guard patrol boats already free to enter Haitian waters. Since 1960 Cuba has denounced the Duvalier regime but made no serious or persistent effort to overthrow it. There are no diplomatic or trade relations, but since the 1970s little overt hostility except for Havana Radio Creole broadcasts, film making by Haitians living in Cuba and, on the Haitian side, the Duvaliers' favorite ploy of denouncing all their foes as communists. Haitians would also probably resent outside interference in their affairs, but they would perhaps accept Cuban or other support to a successor regime. Of greater significance for the future of the regime are the limited political skills of President Jean-Claude Duvalier, the disaffection of the business community, and the possible disruption of the second rural world for the first time since independence because of soil erosion and flight from the land.

The franchise type of political system in Haiti has knitted the interests of rural landholders, middlemen, security forces, and urban business people and industrialists together with the interests of the ruling family. Each group has its method of extracting wealth and exercising power under the Duvalier order. Despite the slogans on tattered banners it is doubtful anyone takes *jean-claudisme* seriously. The noiriste or black power ideology of Dr. Duvalier is weak, but his son has maintained enough blacks in power and has kept the franchise system with the result that key groups are still loyal. However, Jean-Claude Duvalier's presence in the palace is seen in mainly instrumental terms, and, similarly, the president must view the urban and rural elites as instruments for his own security and wealth. Thus, they would desert one another rapidly if they failed in their mutually supportive tasks.

In other words, if the president fails in his task of obtaining foreign assistance, if he upsets the balance of economic and political interests by favoring one group over another without the proper precautions, and if he is unable to control and manipulate the shifting alliances at the top of his government, his supporters will look for someone else to lead the country. His marriage into a mulatto family considered parvenus by other rich mulatto professionals, exporters, and business people undermined the Duvalier color ideology and increased tensions between blacks and mulattoes. Name-calling among school children and jostling mulattoes in markets are among the anecdotal evidence of resentment toward what one black man called ''the return of the brown-skinned people to power with Michele Bennett Duvalier's arrival in the presidential palace.'' On the other hand, we do not wish to exaggerate the black versus brown tensions in Haiti. Racial tensions in Haiti have persisted but have neither completely polarized nor immobilized the society. Often they take the form of petty discriminations which keep Haitians very conscious of color differences but which do not lead to violence. In a part of the world where black versus brown tensions having their origins under slavery are pervasive, Haiti's record of national identity stands out. Haiti is also free of the ethnic conflicts that plague other Caribbean societies such as Guyana, Trinidad, and Tobago, and Surinam where the descendants of African slaves and indentured laborers from India compete for power. Racial intermarriage between blacks and browns is easier and more frequent in Haiti than in interethnic intermarriage in the above societies.

More important are the frequent cabinet changes and reports of conflict between the army, the Leopard unit, and the tontons macoutes, which may serve to keep opposing forces at bay, but may also be a sign of fear and indecisiveness on the part of the president. In the course of 1982 three different men were in the key position of minister of the interior and three more ministers of financial affairs. With each cabinet change a new entourage also came into power, forcing significant numbers of elite Haitians to seek new employment.

The deteriorating economic situation has also called into question presidential political skills. Falling foreign exchange reserves have made it difficult for merchants to respond to demands from creditors. Meanwhile, the government has solicited suppliers credits in order to enter into shaky commercial ventures. Pressures from the IMF to rationalize the fiscal system have alarmed businessmen who fear higher taxes and other measures. The president is seen by some Haitian businessmen as indecisive and vacillating, likely to make concessions to the first group to obtain his attention.

The greatest challenge is the drawing together of the two worlds of Haiti because of the convergence of the other ecological and demographic challenges. The drawing together is first spatial as rural people move to the capital area and are subsequently close to the ruling elites instead of being isolated from them. Second, it is economic because instead of working in agriculture, the former peasants seek work in factories or shops, or they become peddlers, house servants, or beggars. They are much more closely associated with the urban officials and industrialists. Third, it is social as former peasants try to learn some French, give up their rural life style, and become urban workers.

A Marxist would have no trouble predicting that this migration will sooner or later produce an industrial proletariat ready for class conflict and revolution. Knowledge of this class and the more numerous urban poor does not lead to such a facile conclusion. The continuing strength of Voodoo in Port-au-Prince and even in Brooklyn among immigrants is a sign of continuity between rural conservatism and urban living. Another sign is the anticollectivism and desire for cash which transforms itself from raising food and coffee for sale in rural areas to petty commerce in urban areas.

Although the Haitian working-class is small in numbers and lacking in experience and organization, it is not entirely acquiescent. Its most important manifestation in recent years was a spontaneous strike in May 1976 at the foreign-owned cement factory. The strikers emphasized their political loyalty by displaying a national flag and a large photograph of the president. Government representatives pressured the strikers to return to work, promising that some of their salary demands would be met. Gasner Raymond, a young journalist who covered the strike for the weekly *Petit Samedi Soir,* charged intimidation.[22] Although his coverage of the events was published, he was subsequently murdered and his death became a cause célèbre. Since the strike the government has kept a tight lid on any signs of worker activity. Time will tell if the author of a letter to Gasner's newspaper was correct: "Gasner is not dead, he is alive."[23]

Leaving the land opens Haitians up to new experiences, and they must gain some new expectations about what life can offer. Religion and individualism are not absolute barriers to radical change. Neither Confucianism nor family solidarity prevented the victory of the communist movement in China. Change will come although its form is unclear. The traditional elite method of control will not be adequate to a challenge, which will probably be different from the challenge to rulers in other Caribbean states because Haiti's experience and culture are different.

POLITICAL RESPONSES

The regime has three principal political responses at its disposition. The first is to maintain the status quo. Jean-Claude Duvalier rules by franchise but has substantially reduced the fear, insecurity, and random violence that characterized the reign of his father. Haiti has never been a Stalinist or Nazi-type totalitarian state although the black power ideology is national socialist in nature. Under François Duvalier the repression was quite haphazard, unpredictable, and inefficient or wasteful. Police struck out indiscriminately because they did not possess the types of information about citizens that a totalitarian state would have, and, as a result, the idea of political subversion was poorly defined. Any gesture or statement could be interpreted by police forces, who were themselves worried about being spied upon and denounced, as a political threat to the regime. Under Jean-Claude Duvalier urban and rural middle classes feel more secure. Generalized terror has subsided because the police and VSN strike more selectively. Merchants, exporters, and professionals who avoid politics or political commentary run little risk of murder or imprisonment. Small rural landholders, farmers, and the urban poor are still subject to harassment and worse from police and merchants who want their land.

Through the judicious rotation of elites in office, use of appointments and patronage, control over the media and all channels of political expression, and cordial relations with the United States and other foreign powers, the status quo continues to work. Haiti is not nearly so isolated as it was during the 1962–71 period. The carrot and the stick are still the tools of the regime, but there is slightly more carrot, and the stick is not openly brandished at all times.

Another response which has been intermittently explored by Jean-Claude Duvalier involves a broadening of the regime to coopt the urban middle-class groups. Exporters, entrepreneurs, and assembly industry managers and owners have been encouraged to share in new enterprises which also involve speculation in food. The labor force is kept obedient by the police, and both low wages and absence of restrictions on the use of the environment increase profits.[24] The symbolic attempts at black-brown unity, the 1983 municipal elections, the occasional criticism in the press and on the radio, and the agreement to receive the Pope in 1983 are all measures designed to encourage urban middle-class support. So are the gestures under external foreign aid donor pressure to allow Haitian technocrats to reform the customs administration or other aspects of the crippled bureaucracy. Most of these gestures involve limited political risks while drawing some favorable domestic and foreign response. They are essentially openings toward the center or center-right in a narrowly based regime too dependent in the past for its own good on coercion.

Since the demand for middle-class political participation in Haiti is unknown, these gestures often provoke more of a response that the regime wants. It fears that one elected independent legislator or mayor may be the tip of the iceburg, or a few technocrats turned loose in the Ministry of Finance may uncover important secrets. Its own insecurities and fears prompt the regime to terminate or abort liberalizing gestures, as in the harsh treatment accorded in 1979 and 1980 to moderate political dissidents and journalists. Its reaction to any uncontrolled dissent, no matter how mild, is to retreat to the zero-sum rules of Haitian politics and to act harshly and quickly to end the perceived threat. Although there would appear to be ample room to cultivate the middle class with specific political measures without risking power, the regime has yet to learn how to do this with any degree of skill.

A third response was relied on primarily by Dr. Duvalier. He was a master at mobilizing the black masses and using their coerced support to threaten his foes among the mulatto elite. For instance he symbolically legitimized Voodoo by reportedly becoming a priest himself, practicing rituals, and attacking the Christian churches. He widely used Creole in his speeches and suggested its use in schools. He established national organizations and an ideology; he dispensed favors to seek rural support among blacks hoping to join the middle classes. Jean-Claude Duvalier is much less a man of the people, demagogue, or rural mobilizer. He consented to a limited use of Creole in the schools, but then changed course in response to elite and middle-class qualms. He has made his peace with the Catholic church and kept his distance from Voodoo practicioners. His feeble party and jean-claudist ideology lack the mass appeal of his father. Jean-Claude Duvalier does not know or understand the rural milieu as his father did as an ethnographer and physician. He is probably hoping an alliance with urban elites plus enlarged foreign aid programs will fill the gap, but disaffection among the rural middleman, Madan Saras, and petty traders, who benefited from ties with François Duvalier and the tontons macoutes, would be very dangerous for the regime.

NOTES

1. Suzanne Comhaire-Sylvain, *Le roman de Bouqui* (Port-au-Prince: Imprimerie du Collége Vertiéres, 1940), pp. 136–37.

2. Georges Anglade, *L'espace haïtien* (Montreal: Editions de Alizés, 1981), pp. 95–102.

3. Joseph Grunwald, economist, Brookings Institution, Washington, D.C., Personal communications, 15 November 1982.

4. Fritz Pierre-Louis, *Géologie d'Haïti* (Paris: eds. Ecole, 1971), pp. 9–13.

5. Letter reproduced in *Haïti-Observateur*, 6–13 August 1982, pp. 4,6.

6. Aaron Lee Segal, "Haiti," in *Population Policies in the Caribbean*, ed. Aaron Lee Segal (Lexington: Lexington Books, 1975), pp. 177–215.

7. G. Berggren, I.G. Rawson, "Family Structure, Child Lactation and Nutritional Disease in Rural Haiti," *Environmental Child Health* 19 (September 1973):288–98.

8. James Allman and John May, "Fertility, Mortality, Migration, and Family Planning in Haiti," *Population Studies* 33 (1982):505–21.

9. Ibid, pp. 513–14.

10. Uli Locher, Professor of Sociology, McGill University. Statement made at symposium, "Haiti: Present State and Future Prospects," Wingspread Foundation, Racine, Wisconsin, September 25, 1982.

11. Segal, "Haiti," pp. 177–215.

12. Allman and May, "Fertility, Mortality," pp. 515–21. The estimates are by the authors based on the data in the article by Allman and May.

13. "Report of the Commission of Inquiry apointed under article 26...," (Geneiva: ILO, 1983), pp. 35–36.

14. Georges Anglade, *Espace et liberté en Haïti* (Montreal: ERCE and CRC, 1982), pp. 21–22.

15. The National Council of Economic Development Planning (CONADEP) was established in the early 1960s.

16. Andy Rosenblatt, "Black Market Feeds on Aid for the Hungry," *Miami Herald*, 19 December 1982; reproduced in *Haïti Observateur*, 31 December–6 January 1983, p. 13.

17. Robert Debs Heinl, Jr. and Nancy Gordon Heinl, *Written in Blood: The Story of the Haitian People, 1492–1971* (Boston: Houghton Mifflin, 1978), pp. 585–667.

18. Jean Price-Mars, *La vocation de l'élite* (1919; reprint ed., Port-au-Prince: Fardin, 1976), p. 69.

19. René Depestre, *Bonjour et adieu à la négritude* (Paris: Robert Lafont, 1980), pp. 222–23.

20. John Rothchild, "Poet-Actor Richard Brisson dreamed of a better life for his fellow Haitians. Then everything went wrong." *Rolling Stone*, June 10, 1982, pp. 15–18. In March 1982, Roland Magloire and Benjamin Weissberg led another

invasion attempt. See Art Harris, "The Fizzle: Alleged Plot Against Haiti Ended in Choppy Seas," *The Washington Post*, 23 March 1982, p. A9.

21. The Hector Riobé brigade is named after a man who led a guerilla operation against Dr. Duvalier in 1963. Riobé was killed at Kenscoff, in the mountains above the capital.

22. Gasner Raymond, "Les ouvriers de Ciment d'Haïti bouge," *Le Petit Samedi Soir*, 15–21 May 1976, p. 19.

23. *Le Petit Samedi Soir*, 5–11 June 1976, p. 3.

24. Georges Anglade says that patterns of investment and use of the environment in Haiti are an "ecological scandal." Anglade, *Espace et liberté*, p. 25.

7

CONCLUSION: HAITI ALONE

Haiti is a pariah state. While charitable organizations work enthusiastically, comparatively few foreign investors, tourists, and analysts work and travel there. This example of political failure and pervasive poverty inspires feelings of avoidance, disdain, and shame. Only Haitian art, writing, and crafts draw praise abroad. Sometimes, the entrepreneur, visitor, or social scientist who expresses interest in the republic is accused of complicity with the regime and even of enjoying the sight of black suffering.

In many ways Haiti deserves condemnation,[1] but avoidance, and misunderstanding about this country cannot be justified. Nor will it ever help Haitians who are one of the most interesting, attractive, and creative populace in the Caribbean. They and their government are similar in certain ways to other Third World countries, but much contemporary analysis of tropical lands is not helpful to the understanding of Haiti. Often this analysis is addressed to recently independent countries rather than one on its own for almost two centuries. It fails to allow for culture and religion, two factors that are critical in Haitian history. Then there is the focus on ethnicity and cultural and political pluralism which does not world's first black republic.[2]

Haiti's historical experience of a century of intense capita colonialism, and European settlement, followed by a sponta cessful slave uprising, 111 years of isolation and misrule, 19 years of U.S. occupation, and then the development of a franchise system of government, has no close counterparts or analogues anywhere else in the world. Successful slave uprisings on a national scale defeating a colonial power are not to be found in other areas. The establishment of the black republic of Liberia by freed American slaves or the colony of Sierra Leone by ex-British slaves were not the products of nineteenth-century slave revolts but of white emancipationist efforts.

Haiti's experience also differs fundamentally from that of the few traditional societies such as Thailand or Ethiopia which were not transformed by colonial rule. Haiti is the product of a New World synthesis of cultures and values in which what has come by way of Africa and Europe has been vitally transformed.

Like Haiti, other Caribbean societies were founded through colonization which destroyed the indigenous precolonial peoples. Jamaica and Surinam in particular had a series of slave uprisings which led to communities of freed slaves being established in the interior.[3] Yet these maroon runaway slave societies never sought nor attained national liberation. They remained isolated, remote, rural enclaves of the descendants of freed slaves. It was not until 1960 that Jamaica gained its national independence and Surinam in 1976, and in each case independence came through elections and peacefully negotiated transfers of power to elites created by the colonial system.

Haiti's historical experience is singularly different from the rest of the Caribbean.[4] Its independence in 1804 precedes the other island-states, in some cases by over 150 years. It involved no peaceful or parliamentary transfer of power. The plantation slave economy and society ended bloodily by a revolution. Elsewhere slavery held on until 1832 in the British possessions, 1848 in the French islands, and as late as 1868 in Cuba, Puerto Rico, and the Dominican Republic. Formal emancipation did not end the plantation system in these other countries, as indentured laborers were recruited from India, China, and Indonesia during the second half of the nineteenth century to work on the estates.[5] Race remains an issue in much of the Caribbean in ways little known in Haiti.

While many Third World countries struggle with questions on national identity and culture, these were largely resolved in Haiti. Haitians know who they are and readily identify with their art, music, religions, cuisine, games, and Creole language. The reaction to the U.S. occupation solidified the feelings of national identity of the elite sixty years ago; the peasants were ever sure of themselves. Illiterate Creole-speaking Haitians regard

the French Antillean islands of Guadeloupe and Martinique as still populated by "slaves" unlike the free albeit poorer Haitians. Most Haitians,
including the elites, share to some degree in the second world which provides lasting cultural identity. The Haitian experience also differs significantly from that of Latin America.[6] Nineteenth-century independence for
Latin America was the product of locally born elites outlasting in war and
peace a weakened Spain. Independence was not born of slave revolts,
populist causes, or popular insurrections. The Bolívars and San Martíns
waged war in the name of countries that had yet to come into existence,
emotionally or politically. No wonder then that the subsequent nineteenth-
century history in most of the newly independent states is one of strug-
gles between church and state, liberals and conservatives, region and
region, and on occasion government versus government. It is not until the
twentieth century that the urban and rural masses appear in Latin American
history with the Mexican Revolution, populist movements in Brazil, Argentina, and Chile, and other developments. Haiti has known neither the
twentiety-century industrial revolution and emerging social classes of much
of Latin America nor the slow struggle to achieve a sense of national
identity.

The lack of historical analogies is reflected in the inappropriate fit of
various doctrines to the Haitian case. Marxists find in Haiti self-employed
peasants rather than feudalism and large landowners. The industrial workers are less than 10 percent of the working force and signs of a class struggle are few. The destruction of Haiti's plantation slavery brought mass
private landholding.

The dependency theories of some students of Latin America find
combinations of multinational corporations, the U.S. government, and local
business and political elites keeping societies economically and politically
dependent. This view misses the real and deep strength of Haitian nationalism. During the 1960s the Duvalier regime defied Washington, forfeited
much of its foreign aid, and espoused a maximum independence. (Haitian
economists Giovanni Caprio and Philippe Rouzier insist that Haiti was and
still is dependent on world coffee markets, however.) In the 1970s and
1980s private investment in Haiti is largely limited to short-term profit
maximizing assembly industries. There is no evidence that these firms
exercise extensive influence on Haitian policy except in pursuit of their
narrow interests. Similarly, in spite of U.S. predominance in Haitian
foreign trade and aid, the U.S. government has been unable over many
years successfully to pressure the Haitian government into making administrative or other reforms. The U.S. ambassador to Haiti is not more impor-

tant than the president. The dependency theory overlooks more than it explains.

Another theory of students of Latin America, that of "bureaucratic authoritarianism," simply does not fit Haiti.[7] It is used to explain the military governments of Argentina, Brazil, and Chile with their close involvement of the private and public sectors, the technocratic emphases of the military, the pressures for rapid economic growth with little concern for distribution, and the constraints on an open political process. Few of Haiti's political or economic institutions operate as institutions rather than personal avenues. Haiti has neither the bureaucracy nor the kind of authoritarianism that has emerged in Latin America.

More mainstream concepts also run into difficulties when applied to Haiti. Theories of economic development do not explain an economy which has been stagnant or regressing for many years. One needs the tools of microeconomics to understand why farmers retain machete and hoe technologies, how choices are made concerning plots and cultigens, and how rural labor is allocated.

Current theories of political development are not much help either.[8] They tend to emphasize political legitimacy, national identity, changes in attitudes, and political behavior that are much more useful explanatory devices for a newly independent country than for Haiti. For example, Haiti is not a single-party regime; it has never been one. Nor has Haiti experienced a pure military government with the military occupying most major government posts. The Haitian army has lacked competence and respect although individual military men dominated politics until the U.S. occupation. Haiti is that irony of a "soft state" with weak political and bureaucratic institutions but a strong national and cultural identity, a combination that defies the models of how political development should occur in the Third World.

A further irony is that Haiti should be the ideal model for those who believe private enterprise is the key to development. The Haitian government welcomes investors with a broad range of incentives. Its own share in the economy is limited and, until recent risky initiatives, there is little interest in state capitalism. Workers are hardworking, easily trained and loyal, wages are low, and trade unions not tolerated. Haitians at all levels are shrewd entrepreneurs, and private property is highly regarded. The American dollar is legal currency, the National Bank follows antiinflationary policies, and there are no exchange controls or restrictions on remittances of profits. Private enterprise is a way of life in rural Haiti. It operates in terms of many transactions and minuscule rates of return.

Injections of credit and technology are needed so that rural capitalists can afford to take greater risks. At present staying with existing technologies and practices makes eminent sense to rural capitalists who can hardly afford to lose a crop or harvest.[9]

However, Haiti is no Singapore, Taiwan, or even Barbados. It is a place for investors who want to make money quickly, but this means dealing with corruption and inefficient bureaucracies and many other problems. These investments, thought not as important as in other states, are employing Haitians and providing some skills training. But they are manifestly not transforming Haiti.

In the long run, foreign and local private enterprise have limited influence. Public, not private, funds must be spent on nutrition, education, roads, telecommunications, and other services in order to raise productivity. Foreign investors are wary of such low return expenditures. Reynolds Aluminum decided to build its own roads and port, but the result was an enclave isolated from the rest of the country.

TRENDS

Whatever the political and economic evolution of Haiti certain basic trends and tendencies are likely to continue. They will cause difficult problems for any future Haitian government, whatever its nature or orientation.

Regionalism has been suppressed by the Duvaliers but it remains a force in Haiti. The Department of the North with its capital at Cap Haïtien has a strong sense of regional pride and history and has fiercely resented the favoring of the capital. It was no surprise that an independent legislator elected in 1979 and an independent mayor elected in 1983 were at Cap Haïtien.

More and more Haiti is becoming a society built on class rather than color. At the top, brown and black are both prominent and intermarriage is becoming more frequent. Yet the base is overwhelmingly black and there is little social mobility. It is this lack of social mobility that contributes to the continuance of racial attitudes and perceptions. The perceived coincidence of class and color has been eroded but not obliterated. There is a modest, mostly black, urban middle-class and it is this group which is most sensitive to the need for social mobility.

A persistent Haitian concern is over external intervention. Throughout the nineteenth and early twentieth centuries internal disorder served to justify various forms of major power intervention in Haitian affairs. The fiercely independent attitude of the Duvaliers clamps down hard at home to avoid any pretext for intervention. Yet nonmilitary intervention may be needed to force certain changes in Haiti. The need is for a government with sufficient noncoercive authority at home to provide no pretext for external intervention. As a "pirate" regime insisting on absolute sovereignty, the Duvaliers have forfeited much beneficial external aid. A strong sense of identity has not been harnessed to institutions which are too often run on a personalist basis. The pride of the U.S. occupation officials was the institutions they had left in Haitian hands such as the army, public health service, and agricultural education. Within a few years these institutions had disintegrated or withered away. Between powerful loyalties to a rather abstract nation and family Haitians recognize few other binding ties. One can only start institutions by building morale, esprit de corps, job security, and a sense of achievement. Without institution-building Haiti cannot fit ends to means and regain a sense of control over its present and future. One begins with the few institutions like the National Bank that have a degree of continuity and performance and builds on them.

The classic drama of Haitian history has been the prolonged political struggle which results in centralized presidential rule which is then in turn torn apart by coups and factions. Haiti has little experience in the sharing of power, whether between legislature and executive, between regions, and between president and cabinet or judiciary. Coalitions work badly if at all and result in agreement on the need for a strong president. Power then corrupts, strong presidents seek to extend their powers and terms, and the political merry-go-round begins again. This is a problem of weak institutions and lack of legitimacy but is also one of political style and behavior. Haiti does not operate in terms of checks and balances except when a strong president is overthrown. No one has any use for weak presidents. No doubt post-Duvalier the demand will be for a reformist strong president to rectify past grievances. Lacking effective constraints, few Haitian presidents have been able or willing to curb their own appetites for power. Strong presidential rule is what Haiti knows but it has not been best for Haiti.

Our last trend is the perplexing relationship between politics and culture. An original, vibrant culture has thrived for nearly two centuries in spite of politics in both worlds of Haiti. Culture is not coopted. Haitian artists are not subsidized and government support for the arts is minimal. Haitian culture is authentic and its authenticity includes the political dimension in Haitian lives. But it is not always explicitly political and does not seek to back or overthrow regimes or leaders. Haitian art draws no line between body and spirit. One can confidently predict that the richness and breadth of Haitian culture and art will continue, reflecting the political context of the day but also transcending it. It is a culture which enables them to cope with the man-made and natural realities of life.

During the Haitian revolution the genius of Haiti's cultural identity emerged. The core elements are the Creole language, Voodoo beliefs and practices, the value attached to individual landholding, no matter how small the land, enthusiasm for trade, cultural creativity, and race pride. During the nineteenth century the first world of Haiti left people in the second free to till their plots, to worship as they chose, to make their own marital arrangements, and to use Creole. The elites produced by the revolution and political evolution were content to extract a share of the peasants' produce without demanding their loyalty.

Stagnation, inflation, ecological degradation, growing landlessness are now the threats to Haitian rural society limiting its ability to produce for the elites. New forces may be released by these processes, and it is not unlikely that they will operate in peculiarly Haitian ways on Haitian realities.

Haitian political realities are not black or Caribbean or Third World. They are human realities commanding our attention no matter how much we would like to avoid them. All of us are threatened by any consistent and officially sanctioned inhumanity. A Germany under the Nazi boot, a Cambodia under the Khmer Rouge, a Stalinist gulag, and legalized apartheid or segregation cannot be isolated as exotic white, black, or yellow aberrations and then ignored. The example of a government which successfully oppresses or allows the oppression and exploitation of its own people is an encouragement to other forces and leaders of darkness. Organized societies everywhere are threatened by the Haitian example.

For 180 years politics have failed to bring about a just order in Haiti. Hobbes's war of all against all has been institutionalized in state and economic structures. This particular example of inversion of the social contract is a warning. Now let us say we are all Haitians.

NOTES

1. Michael Hooper has documented the systematic violation of human rights in his "Violations of Human Rights in Haiti, June 1981–September 1982." A report to the Organization of American States, (Washington, D.C.: OAS, 1982).

2. Crawford Young, *The Politics of Cultural Pluralism* (Madison: Wisconsin: University of Wisconsin, 1976) pp. 3–23.

3. Bryan Edwards, "Observations on the Maroon Negroes of the Island of Jamaica," and Silvia W. DeGroot, "The Bush Negro Chiefs Visit Africa: Diary

of an Historic Trip,'' in *Maroon Societies,* ed. Richard Price (New York: Anchor Press, 1973), pp. 227–246, 389–99.

4. Eric Williams, *From Columbus to Castro (History of the Caribbean 1492–1969)* (London: Andre Deutsch, 1970). Both as a historian and as Prime Minister of Trinidad and Tobago, Dr. Williams considered the Haitian revolution to have left Haiti with a unique character in the region.

5. K.O. Laurence, *Immigration into the West Indies in the 19th Century* (Barbados: Caribbean Universities Press, 1971), pp. 20–45.

6. Magnus Mörner, *Race Mixture in the History of Latin America* (Boston: Little Brown, 1967). Mörner argues that during the nineteenth century most Latin American national identities were weak in societies still racially stratified.

7. Guillermo O'Donnell, ''Reflections on the Pattern of Change in the Bureaucratic-Authoritarian State,'' *Latin American Research Review* 13 (1978):3–38.

8. Young, *The Politics of Cultural Pluralism* pp. 66–98.

9. Theodore Schultz, *Investing in People* (Berkeley: University of California, 1982). Schultz has argued that peasant farmers are rational decision makers, given the constraints and risks associated with their choices.

BIBLIOGRAPHY

Alexis, Jacques Stéphen. *Compère Général Soleil.* 3rd ed. Paris: Gallimard, 1955.

Allman, James, and John May. "Fertility, Mortality, Migration, and Family Planning in Haiti." *Population Studies* 33 (1982):505–21.

Anglade, Georges. *Espace et liberté en Haiti.* Montreal: ERCE and CRC, 1982.

———. *L'espace haïtien.* Montreal: Editions des Alizes, 1981.

Anglade, Georges, Denis Audette, and Rafael Emilio Yunen. *Hispaniola: Les lectures d'une carte murale.* Montreal: Université du Québec, 1982.

Antoine, Jacques C. *Jean Price-Mars and Haiti* Washington: Three Continents Press, 1981.

Beghin, Ivan, William Fougére, and Kendall W. King. *L'aliénation et la nutrition en Haïti.* Paris: Presses Univesitaires de France, 1970.

Berggren, G., and I.G. Rawson. "Family Structure, Child Lactation and Nutritional Diseases in Rural Haiti. *"Environmental Child Health* 19 (September 1973):288–98.

Brinkerhoff, Derick, et al. "Administrative Reform and Plans for Decentralization in Haiti" Report for USAID, Port-au-Prince, November 1981.

"Budget Général de l'Exercice 1981–1982, October 1981–September 1982." *Le Moniteur Officiel* 1 (28 September 1981):77, 93, 95, 106.

Buell, Raymond Leslie. "The American Occupation of Haiti." *Information Service* 5 New York, Foreign Policy Association, (27 November–12 December 1929).

——. "Sugar and the Tariff." *Information Service* 5 New York, Foreign Policy Association (29 May 1929).

Bulletin of the Institut Pédagogique National, Port-au-Prince.

Bulletin Trimestriel De Statistique, Port-au-Prince: IHS.

Calixte, Colonel D.P. *Haiti: The Calvary of a Soldier.* New York, Wendell Malliet, 1939.

Campfort, Gérard. "Enjeu éducatif en Haïti." Unpublished mémoire, Paris: Université de Paris I, 1976.

Caprio, Giovanni. *Haiti: Wirtschaftliche Entwicklung und periphere Gesellschaftsformation.* Frankfurt/Main: Haag und Herchen, 1979.

Castor, Suzy. *La ocupación norteamericana de Haití y sus consecuencias (1915–1934).* Mexico: Siglo Vientiuno, 1971.

Chancy, Max. "Education et développement en Haiti." in *Culture et développement en Haïti,* edited by Emerson Douyon, pp. 135–55. Ottawa: Editions Lemeac, 1972.

Comhaire, Jean L., "The Haitian 'Chef de Section'." *American Anthropologist* 57 (1955):620–23.

Comhaire-Sylvain, Suzanne. *Le roman de Bouqui.* Port-au-Prince: Imprimerie Collège Vertières, 1940.

Cook, Mercer. "Trends in Recent Haitian Literature." *The Journal of Negro History* 32 (April 1947).

Cornevin, Robert. *Haiti.* Paris: Presses universitaires de France, Que sais-je?, 1982.

Courlander, Harold *The Drum and the Hoe: Life and Lore of the Haitian People* Berkeley: University of California, 1974.

Courlander, Harold. *Haiti Singing*. New York: Cooper Sq., 1973.

Dash, J. Michael. *Literature and Ideology in Haiti 1915–1961*. Totowa, New Jersey: Barnes and Noble, 1981.

Delince, Kern. *Armée et politique en Haïti*. Paris: Editions L'Harmattan, 1979.

Denis, Lorimer, and François Duvalier. *Evolution stadiale du Vodou*. Port-au-Prince: Imprimerie de l'Etat, 1944.

———. *Probléme des classes à travers l'histoire d'Haïti*. Port-au-Prince: Collection 'Les Griots', 1948.

Département de l'Education Nationale. *La réforme éducative: Eléments d'information*. Port-au-Prince: Institut Pédagogique Nationale, 1982.

Depestre, René. *Bonjour et adieu à la négritude*. Paris: Robert Lafonte, 1980.

Dorsainvil, J.C. *Manuel d'histoire d'Haïti*. Port-au-Prince: Fréres de l'Instruction Chrétienne, 1934.

Dutcher, Nadine. *The Use of First and Second Languages in Primary Education: Selected Case Studies*. World Bank Staff Working Paper No. 504, January 1982. Washington: World Bank, 1982.

Duvalier, Docteur François. *Mémoires d'un leader du Tiers Monde*. Paris: Hachette, 1969.

Esteban Deive, Carlos. *El Indio, el Negro y la Vida Traditional Dominicana*. Santo Domingo: Museo del Hombre, 1978.

Filostrat, Christian. "The Search for an African Identity in the Caribbean: Genesis and Rise of Haitianism and Negritude." Ph.D. dissertation, Howard University, Washington, D.C. 1978.

Fleischmann, Ulrich. "Entrevue avec Franketienne sur son roman 'Dezafi'." *Derives* (Montreal) (1977):20–21.

———. "Le Créole en voie de devenir une langue littéraire." In *Littératures et langues dialectales françaises,* edited by Dieter Kremer and Hans-Josef Niederehe. Hamburg: Helmut Buske, 1979.

Foster, Charles R. and Albert Valdman (eds) *Haiti: An Interdisciplinary Study* Durham, N.C.: Duke University, 1984 forthcoming.

Gaillard, Roger. *Charlemagne Péralte le Caco.* Les blancs débarquent 1918–1919, vol. 6 (Port-au-Prince: Roger Gaillard, 1982).

——. *Les blancs débarquent: 1915 premier écrasement du Cacoisme.* 2nd ed. Port-au-Prince: Roger Gaillard, 1982.

Garcia-Zamor, Jean-Claude, "Haiti." *Latin America and Caribbean Contemporary Record.* New York: Holmes and Meier, 1983.

——. *La Administracion Publica en Haití.* Guatemala: Editorial Landivar: 1966.

Garrity, Monique. "The Multinational Corporation in Extractive Industries: A Case Study of Reynolds Haitians Mines, Inc." in *Working Papers in Haitian Society and Culture,* edited by Sidney W. Mintz, pp. 183–290. New Haven: Yale University Antilles Research Program, 1975.

Girault, Christian A. *Le commerce du café en Haïti: Habitants, spéculateurs et exportateurs.* Mémoire du Centre d'Etudes de Géographie Tropicale-Bordeaux. Paris: CNRS, 1981.

Grunwald, Joseph, Leslie Delatour, and Karl Voltaire. "Offshore Assembly in Haiti." In *The Internationalization of Industry,* Washington: Brookings, forthcoming.

Haïti-Observateur (New York), weekly.

Heinl, Robert Debs, Jr., and Nancy Gordon Heinl. *Written in Blood: The Story of the Haitian People 1492–1971.* Boston: Houghton Mifflin, 1978.

Herdeck, Donald E., with Maurice A. Lubin, et al. eds. *Caribbean Writers: A Bio-Bibliographical Critical Encyclopedia.* Washington, D.C.: Three Continents Press, 1979.

Herskovits, Melville J. *Life in a Haitian Valley.* Garden City, New York: Doubleday, 1971.

Hippolyte-Manigat, Mirlande, *Haiti and the Caribbean Community: Profile*

of an Applicant and the Problematique of Widening the Integration Movement.
Translated by K.Q. Warner. Kingston, Jamaica: Institute of Social and Economic
Research, University of the West Indies, 1980.

Hoffman, Léon-François *Le roman haïtien: Idéologie et structure* Sher-
brooke, Quebec: Naaman, 1982.

Honorat, Jean-Jacques. *Enquête sur le développement.* Port-au-Prince:
Imprimerie Centrale, 1974.

Hooper, Michael, "Violations of Human Rights in Haiti: A Report of the
Lawyers Committee for International Human Rights to the Organization of
American States." November 1980.

Hurbon, Laënnec. *Culture et dictature en Haïti: L'imaginaire sous contrôle.*
Paris: L'Harmattan, 1979.

International Labor Organization, *Report on Small Enterprises in Haiti.*
Geneva: ILO, 1979.

James, C.L.R. *The Black Jacobins: Toussaint L'Ouverture and the San
Domingo Revolution.* 2nd ed. New York: Random House-Vintage, 1963.

JWK International Corporation. "Coffee Policy Study: Haiti." Damien,
Haiti: Agricultural Policy Project, on contract with AID, 15 April 1976.

Kennedy, Ellen Conroy, trans. and ed. *The Negritude Poets: An Anthology
of Translations from the French.* New York: The Viking Press, 1975.

Labelle, Micheline. *Idéologie de couleur et classes sociales en Haïti.* Montreal: Presses de l'universitée de Montreal, 1978.

Laguerre, Michel S. *Voodoo Heritage.* Beverly Hills: Sage, 1980.

Lahav, Pnina. "The Chef de Section: Structures and Functions of Haiti's
Basic Administrative Institution." In *Working Papers in Haitian Society and Cul-
ture,* edited by Sidney W. Mintz. New Haven: Yale University Antilles Research
Program, 1975, pp. 51–84.

Lemoine, Maurice. *Sucre amer: Esclaves aujourd'hui dans les Caraïbes,*
Paris: Nouvelle Société des Editions Encre, 1981.

Leyburn, James G. *The Haitian People.* New Haven: Yale University Press,
1941. Second Edition, Introduction by Sidney W. Mintz, 1966.

Lofficial, Frantz. *Créole francais: Une fausse querelle-Bilinguisme et reforme de l'enseignement en Haïti*. Lasalle, Quebec: Collectif Paroles, 1979.

Logan, Rayford W. *The Diplomatic Relations of the United States with Haiti 1776–1981*. Chapel Hill: University of North Carolina, 1941.

———. *Haiti and the Dominican Republic*. New York: Oxford, 1968.

Lowenthal, Ira P. "Ritual Performance and Religious Experience: A Service for the Gods in Southern Haiti" *Journal of Anthropological Research* 34, 3, Fall, 1978:392–414.

Lubin, Maurice, with Carlos Saint-Louis. *Panorama de la poésie d'Haïti*. Port-au-Prince: Henri Deschamps, 1950.

Lundhall, Mats. *Man, Land and Markets: Essays on the Haitian Economy*. London and Canberra: Croom Helm, 1983.

———. "Peasant Strategies for Dealing with Population Pressure: The Case of Haiti." *Ibero Americana: Nordic Journal of Latin American Studies* 10 (1981).

———. *Peasants and Poverty*. New York: St. Martin's Press, 1979.

———. "The State of Spatial Economic Research on Haiti: A Selective Survey." *Anthropologica* 22 (1980), pp. 137–56.

Maguire, Robert. *Bottom-Up Development in Haiti*. 2nd ed. Rosslyn, Va.: Inter-American Foundation, April 1981.

Manigat, Charles, Claude Moïse, and Emile Ollivier. *Haiti: Quel développement-Propos sur l' enquête de Jean-Jacques Honorat*. Montreal: Collectif Paroles, 1975.

Manigat, Leslie F. *Haiti of the Sixties, Object of International Concern*. Washington: The Washington Center of Foreign Policy Research, 1964.

Metraux, Alfred. *Haiti: Black Peasants and Their Religion*. London: George Harrup, 1960.

———. Métraux, Alfred. *Le vaudou haïtien*. Paris: Gallimard, 1968.

Mintz, Sidney W. *Caribbean Transformation*. Chicago: Aldine, 1974.

Le Moniteur: Journal Officiel de la Republique d'Haiti.

Moral, Paul. *Le paysan haïtien*. Paris: G.P. Maisonneuve et Larouse, 1961. Reprint. Port-au-Prince, Fardin, 1978.

Morisseau-Leroy, F. *Récolte*. Port-au-Prince: Les Editions Haïtiennes, 1946.

Munro, Dana G. *Intervention and Dollar Diplomacy in the Caribbean 1900– 1921*. 1964. Reprint. Westport, Conn: Greenwood, 1980.

Munro, Dana G. *The United States and the Caribbean Republics*. Princeton: Princeton University Press, 1974.

Murray, Gerald. *Haitian Peasant Control Ridges: The Evolution of Indigenous Erosion Control Technology*. Cambridge: Harvard Institution of International Development, Discussion Paper 86, March 1980.

Nicholls, David. *From Dessalines to Duvalier: Race, Colour and National Independence in Haiti*. Cambridge: Cambridge University Press, 1979.

Ott, Thomas. *The Haitian Revolution*. Knoxville: University of Tennessee Press, 1973.

Le Petit Samedi Soir (Port-au-Prince), weekly.

Pierre-Charles, Gérard. *Haití: La Crisis Ininterrumpida*. Havana: Casa de las Americas, 1978.

Pierre-Charles, Gérard *Radiographie d'une dictature: Haïti et Duvalier* Montreal: Nouvelle Optique, 1973.

Pierre-Louis, Fritz. *Géologie d'Haïti*. Paris: Eds. Ecole, 1971.

Piquion, Dr. René. *Manuél de Negritude*. Port-au-Prince: Henri Deschamps, 1965(?).

Price, Hannibal. *De la réhabilitation de la Race Noire par la République d'Haiti*. Port-au-Prince: Verrollet, 1901.

Price-Mars, Jean. *Ainsi parla l'oncle*. Ottawa: Lemeac, 1973.

——. *La vocation de l'élite*. (Port-au-Prince: Imprimerie Edmond Chenet, 1919.

——. *Lettre ouverte au Dr. René Piquion sur son manuel de la négritude, Le préjugé de couleur est-il la question sociale?* Port-au-Prince: Editions des Antilles, 1967.

"Report of the Commission of Inquiry appointed under article 26 of the Constitution of the International Labour Organisation to examine the observance of certain international labour Conventions by the Dominican Republic and Haiti with respect to the employment of Haitian workers on the sugar plantations of the Dominican Republic," mimeo Geneva: International Labour Office, 1983.

Rodman, Selden. *The Miracle of Haitian Art.* New York: Doubleday, 1974.

Rotberg, Robert I., with Christopher K. Clague. *Haiti: The Politics of Squalor.* Boston: Houghton Mifflin, 1971.

Roumain, Jacques. *La montagne ensorcelée.* Port-au-Prince: Collection Indigène, 1931. Reprint. Port-au-Prince: Ateliers Fardin, n.d.

———. *Masters of the Dew.* Translated by Mercer Cook and Langston Hughes. New York: Reynal and Hitchcock, 1947.

Rouzier, Philippe. *Echange et développement (Cadre théorique pour une alternative.)* Ottawa: Universite d'Ottawa, 1981.

Rubin, Vera, and Richard P. Schaedel, eds. *The Haitian Potential: Research and Resources of Haiti.* New York: Teachers College Press, 1975.

Schmidt, Hans. *The United States Occupation of Haiti 1915–1934.* New Brunswick: Rutgers University Press, 1971.

Segal, Aaron Lee, ed. *Population Policies in the Caribbean.* Lexington, Mass.: D.C. Heath, 1975.

Standing Committee on External Affairs and National Defense. *Canada's Relations with the Caribbean and Central America: Report to the House of Commons, 29 July 1982.* Hull, Quebec: Canadian Government Publishing Centre, 1982.

Stepick, Alex, with Dale Frederick Swartz. *Haitian Refugees in the U.S.* London: Minority Rights Group, 1982.

US/AID/Haiti. *Country Development Strategy FY 1983–87.* Port-au-Prince: AID Jan. 1981. Mimeographed.

United States General Accounting Office. *Assistance to Haiti: Barriers, Recent Program Changes and Future Options.* Washington: GAO, ID 82–13, February 22, 1982, p. 1.

Valdman, Albert. ''Education Reform and the Instrumentalization of the Vernacular in Haiti.'' In *Issues in International Bilingual Education: The Role of the Vernacular*, edited by Beverly Hartford, Albert Valdman, and Charles R. Foster, pp. 139–70. New York: Plenum Press, 1982.

Weinstein, Brian. *The Civic Tongue: Political Consequences of Language Choices*. New York: Longman, 1983.

Wood, Harold A. *Northern Haiti: Land, Land Use, and Settlement*. Toronto: University of Toronto, 1963.

de Young, Maurice. *Man and Land in the Haitian Economy*. Gainesville: University of Florida Press, 1958.

Zuvenkas, Clarence. *Land Tenure, Income, and Employment in Rural Haiti: A Survey*. Washington: Agency for International Development, May 1978.

INDEX

ABOUT THE AUTHORS

Educated at Yale, Harvard and the University of Paris, **Brian Weinstein** has taught political science at Howard University since 1966. He is the author of *Gabon: Nation-Building on the Ogooue,* (1967), *Eboue* (1972), *Introduction to African Politics,* with L. Rubin (2nd edition, 1977), and *The Civic Tongue: Political Consequences of Language Choices* (1983).

Aaron Segal is a professor of political science at the University of Texas at El Paso. Educated at Occidental College, Oxford University, where he was a Rhodes Scholar, and the University of California at Berkeley, he has written extensively on Africa, the Caribbean, and Latin America. His previous books include *The Politics of Caribbean Economic Integration, Population Policies in the Caribbean,* and *The Traveler's Africa.*

POLITICS IN LATIN AMERICA
A HOOVER INSTITUTION SERIES

General Editor, **Robert Wesson**

SOCIALISM, LIBERALISM, AND DICTATORSHIP
IN PARAGUAY
Paul H. Lewis

PANAMANIAN POLITICS:
From Guarded Nation to National Guard
Steve C. Ropp

BOLIVIA: Past, Present, and Future of Its Politics
Robert J. Alexander

MEXICAN POLITICS: The Containment of Conflict
Martin C. Needler

DEMOCRACY IN COSTA RICA
Charles D. Ameringer

BRAZIL IN TRANSITION
Robert Wesson and David V. Fleischer

VENEZUELA: Politics in a Petroleum Republic
David E. Blank